BrightRED Study Guide

CfE HIGHER

ACCOUNTING

Helen Lang and William Reynolds

BrightRED
PUBLISHING

First published in 2017 by:
Bright Red Publishing Ltd
1 Torphichen Street
Edinburgh
EH3 8HX

A CIP record for this book is available from the British Library

ISBN 978-1-906736-89-7

With thanks to:
PDQ Digital Media Solutions Ltd (layout) and Ivor Normand (edit)

Cover design and series book design by Caleb Rutherford – e i d e t i c

Acknowledgements
Every effort has been made to seek all copyright holders. If any have been overlooked, then Bright Red Publishing will be delighted to make the necessary arrangements.

Permission has been sought from all relevant copyright holders and Bright Red Publishing are grateful for the use of the following:

Images licensed by Ingram Image on pages 6, 8, 16, 32, 38, 44, 45, 46, 47, 49, 51, 56, 57, 58, 64, 65, 66, 70, 71, 72, 74, 76, 79, 84, 87, 88, 89, 90, 91 and 92; Foreign and Commonwealth Office (CC BY 2.0)[1] (p 7); whitemay/iStock.com (p 7); Logo reproduced with permission of Thomas Tunnock Limited (p 7); Walmart (CC BY 2.0)[1] (p 8); jam_90s (CC BY 2.0)[1] (p 8); Caleb Rutherford – e i d e t i c (p 10); supergenijalac/iStock.com (p 32); Photoblaz/iStock.com (p 33); Olavssilis/Dreamstime (p 80); billadrian96 (CC BY-SA 2.0)[2] (p 88).

[1] (CC BY 2.0) http://creativecommons.org/licenses/by/2.0/
[2] (CC BY-SA 2.0) https://creativecommons.org/licenses/by-sa/2.0/

Printed and bound in the UK by Martins the Printers.

MIX
Paper from
responsible sources
FSC® C013254

CONTENTS

INTRODUCTION

PREPARING FINANCIAL ACCOUNTING INFORMATION

PREPARING MANAGEMENT ACCOUNTING INFORMATION

INDEX

INTRODUCTION

INTRODUCING HIGHER ACCOUNTING

Accounting is often defined as 'the language of business'. Accountants aim to collect, classify, organise, analyse, present and communicate financial information to the owners of a business and other interested parties.

TYPES OF ACCOUNTING

Financial accounting focuses on presenting general-purpose financial statements (Income Statements and Statements of Financial Position) mainly for use by stakeholders outside of the business. These financial statements must be prepared in line with Statements of Standard Accounting Practice.

Management accounting involves providing the management of a business with the information they need to keep the business 'financially healthy'. This information is not normally distributed outside of the business. Much of this information will be based on estimates and projections based on various assumptions. Examples include the preparation of production budgets and estimating the selling price for quoting new jobs.

Today, many of the recording, organising and presenting aspects of accounting have been automated as a result of the advances in computer technology.

This Higher Study Guide will help you to understand and interpret both financial and management accounting information and will equip you with the necessary skills to undertake a range of accounting tasks. It will also help you to develop and apply skills for learning, skills for work and skills for life.

HIGHER COURSE CONTENT

The Higher course contains two main units of study:

Preparing financial accounting information (Higher)

This unit will focus on the role of financial accounting. Financial accounting is concerned with reporting on the past, chiefly for the benefit of the business owners, trade payables and potential investors. In this unit, you will develop the skills, knowledge and understanding to prepare financial statements (Income Statements and Statements of Financial Position) for a range of business organisations including partnerships, private and public limited companies and manufacturing organisations. You will also develop the accounting skills relating to the interpretation and analysis of financial information to enable you to report on an organisation's current financial position using investment ratios. A study of investment appraisal will also enable you to compare investment options available to a business and to offer financial advice based on accounting data.

This unit will also highlight the importance of International Accounting Standards as well as key accounting concepts and conventions.

Preparing management accounting information (Higher)

Management accounting is concerned with the future and seeks to provide internal management with the accounting information it needs to run the business on a day-to-day basis. In this unit, you will develop the skills, knowledge and understanding to carry out a range of costing techniques including overhead analysis, job costing, process costing, service costing and the preparation of budgets. You will gain an understanding of the impact that management accounting has on making decisions about the planning, control and future success of a business organisation. In particular, you will consider how a business can make decisions that will maximise profits under conditions of a limiting factor.

COURSE ASSESSMENT

Internal assessment

Each of the two units above will have a formal unit assessment. Unit assessments will require you to prepare accounting statements as well as to be able to apply knowledge and understanding of key accounting concepts. All internal unit assessments will be undertaken in accordance with SQA assessment specifications. All unit assessments will be marked as a pass or a fail and will be subject to external verification by the SQA.

External assessment: question paper

The question paper will have 100 marks, and you will be expected to attempt all questions. This will be an end-of-course examination paper set by the SQA. The examination paper has two sections:

- Section 1 tends to be made up of one 40-mark question testing computational and theoretical skills.

- Section 2 is worth 60 marks and tends to contain a larger number of smaller computational and theoretical questions.

The question paper will be a closed-book assessment, and you will not know in advance what areas of the course content will be assessed.

External assessment: assignment

The assignment will have 50 marks. It will require you to work through a series of integrated tasks to prepare accounting information and financial statements. You will also be required to use accounting information to aid decision-making, to analyse an organisation's financial position or to make recommendations for the future.

Topics within the assignment can come from any areas outlined in the course specification; and one task will be required to be completed using spreadsheet software. You will be required to make use of complex spreadsheet formulae such as conditional formatting, for example IF statements.

To ensure you are well prepared for both the question paper and the assignment, tasks in this Study Guide should be completed manually and using spreadsheet software.

The assignment will be completed within presenting centres, but marked externally by the SQA.

 **DON'T FORGET**

To gain an overall award in Higher Grade Accounting, you must secure a pass in all of the units as well as the external course assessment.

HOW THIS BOOK CAN HELP YOU

This Study Guide (supported by the Digital Zone) explains clearly and precisely all the financial and management accounting concepts you need to know and understand to pass the internal and external elements of the Higher Accounting course. It also has a wide range of challenging tasks and activities which provide you with the opportunity to develop your accounting skills.

The Study Guide will also ensure that the following generic skills for learning, life and work are fully developed:

Numeracy	ICT	Decision-making	Presentation	Analysing
Evaluating	Thinking	Employability	Enterprise	Analytical

 ONLINE

Go to the Digital Zone to find out more about International Accounting Standards.

International Accounting Standards (IAS)

Adoption of International Accounting Standards (IAS) requires a change in the terminology used in the preparation of the final accounts of business organisations. This Study Guide makes use of International Accounting Standards (IAS) terminology throughout.

PREPARING FINANCIAL ACCOUNTING INFORMATION

THE ROLE OF THE FINANCIAL ACCOUNTANT

INTRODUCTION

Financial accounting is concerned mainly with the recording function (often referred to as double-entry book-keeping) and the preparation of final accounting statements (Income Statements and Statements of Financial Position) for different types of business organisations.

The objectives of financial accounting

The main objectives of financial accounting are:

1. To ensure that the preparation of financial statements complies with the law (Companies Act), particularly for public limited companies.

2. To prepare a historical record of the financial affairs of a business – financial accounting statements are prepared at the end of an accounting period.

3. To provide financial accounting statements for both internal and external purposes and to make these statements available to shareholders, lenders and other stakeholders.

4. To ensure that financial accounting statements comply with the principles outlined in statements of accounting standards laid down by professional accounting bodies.

5. To ensure that financial accounting statements/information shows the stewardship of the organisation and the accountability of the board of directors to shareholders and other stakeholders.

6. To provide financial accounting information to the management of a business organisation for decision-making purposes.

Duties of a financial accountant

The financial accountant will undertake a range of duties including the following:

1. Reporting to the owners of a business the effects of managerial decisions on the financial performance of the business.

2. Keeping accurate records of the daily financial transactions of the business.

3. Checking the financial records to maintain accuracy and reduce fraud.

4. Preparing periodic financial statements – Income Statements and Statements of Financial Position.

5. Preparing accounts for auditing and publication as and if required.

6. Ensuring that the business is adhering to and operating within the rules laid down by government legislation and/or professional accounting bodies.

7. Taxation calculations.

8. Ratio analysis to compare the current performance of the business with past performance or to the performance of similar businesses.

contd

Disadvantages of financial accounting

1. Financial accounting is historical and deals with operations which have already occurred. In a business, you can control what is happening or about to happen, but you cannot change what has already happened.

2. Financial accounting is concerned with the whole business. A business may make an annual profit for the year of £250,000 from manufacturing and selling 3 separate products, but this does not tell us whether all 3 products are making a profit.

 **DON'T FORGET**

Financial accounting information is historical.

PREPARING FINANCIAL ACCOUNTING INFORMATION

Introduction to company accounts

Companies can be divided into two types:

1. A **public** limited company, which is shown as **plc**.

2. A **private** limited company, which is shown as **Ltd**.

A public limited company issues **shares** on the Stock Exchange. Investors buy these, and this forms the company's equity. A private company does not sell shares to the public. It is usually owned by a few people (shareholders), usually close friends or family.

A limited company (both plc and Ltd) means that the liability of the shareholders is limited to the amount they have invested, that is, to the number of shares they own. A sole trader or a partner in a partnership agreement has **unlimited liability**, and so his/her personal possessions (for example, personal assets such as their house or car) can be seized should their business fail.

If a company has a fixed equity of £100,000, then only £100,000 can be claimed by the creditors although the actual debts may be much greater.

 **DON'T FORGET**

Plc indicates a public limited company; Ltd indicates a private limited company.

Marks & Spencer is an example of a public limited company

Tunnock's is an example of a private limited company

 ONLINE

Find exercises on company accounts at www.brightredbooks.net

 ONLINE TEST

Test yourself on preparing financial accounting information online at www.brightredbooks.net

 THINGS TO DO AND THINK ABOUT

Specimen exam-style questions

1. Outline the main objectives of financial accounting.

2. Describe three duties that may be undertaken by a financial accountant.

3. Discuss the limitations of financial accounting information.

EQUITY, PROFITS AND DEBENTURES

Shareholders' meeting

Board of directors

EQUITY

Equity for a public limited company is raised by selling shares to the public. There are two main types of shareholders:

1. Preference shareholders
2. Ordinary shareholders.

Preference shareholders have first claim on any profit made by the company. The drawback is that these shares carry a fixed rate of interest, usually quite low – about 4–5%. These shares are attractive to investors who are not keen on taking risks. Such investors have no voting rights at annual general meetings (AGMs) and so have no real say in the running of the company. However, if a plc is wound up, preference shareholders will have priority on receiving their shareholding (equity) compared with ordinary shareholders.

Ordinary shareholders are the most common type. These shares have no fixed rate of dividend, and the shareholders receive an equal share of any remaining profit after preference shareholders have received their dividend. If a company has a particularly good year, then a dividend of (for example) 10% could be declared to the ordinary shareholders. This type of share is often favoured by those investors who are willing to take a risk in order to achieve higher returns on their investment in the business. Unlike preference shareholders, ordinary shareholders have voting rights and so can influence the behaviour of the board of directors.

A **public limited company** is therefore owned collectively by the shareholders, and a board of directors is appointed to represent the shareholders and to oversee the management of the company on behalf of the many shareholders. This is often referred to as the **stewardship function**.

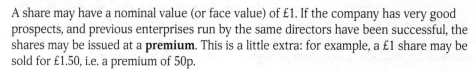

When applying to form a company, the founders must state what they consider to be the desirable sum for equity. If this is approved by the Department of Trade and Industry, it becomes the authorised equity.

Share premium

A share may have a nominal value (or face value) of £1. If the company has very good prospects, and previous enterprises run by the same directors have been successful, the shares may be issued at a **premium**. This is a little extra: for example, a £1 share may be sold for £1.50, i.e. a premium of 50p.

The collective premium on shares is recorded in a **share premium account**, and this is shown in the reserves section of the Statement of Financial Position.

Characteristics of a Public Limited Company	Characteristics of a Private Limited Company
1. Public limited companies are owned by shareholders and run by an elected board of directors	1. Private limited companies are usually smaller than a plc and are family-run businesses
2. Shareholders have limited liability: liability is limited to the value of their shares	2. Shareholder liability is limited to the value of their shares, and personal assets cannot be seized by creditors (trade payables)
3. There is a minimum of 7 shareholders/members and a limitless number of shareholders/members	3. A minimum of 2 shareholders are required to form a private limited company; the maximum number of shareholders is 50

contd

4. Shares of a public limited company are transferable and are bought and sold on the stock market	4. Transfer of share ownership may only take place with agreement of other shareholders – so control of the company cannot be lost
5. A plc is not affected by the death of a shareholder – a plc will continue to exist even if its shareholders change	5. Shares are not available for sale to the public on the stock market, and additional shares can only be sold with agreement of existing shareholders
6. A plc is regulated by law and must publish its annual accounts	6. Small and medium-sized companies are not required to publish final accounts
7. Large amounts of equity can be raised as shares and sold on the stock exchange to the public	7. There is no requirement to hold an annual general meeting
8. A minimum of £50,000 share equity is required to form a plc	8. There are no minimum or maximum share equity requirements
9. Outsiders can take over ownership of the plc if they can purchase 50% of the shares	9. Growth may be limited because maximum shareholders allowed is only 50
10. A plc will pay corporation tax on profits	10. Shareholders will receive dividends on their share equity

PROFITS

Once a company has paid all expenses, the directors decide on how much to declare as a dividend.

Although preference shareholders have prior claim on any profits, the directors may decide not to issue a dividend that year. Some companies may have **cumulative** preference shares, which means that investors can claim back any unpaid dividend from previous years.

Once the preference shareholders have been paid, the dividend is declared, approved and paid to the ordinary shareholders.

Not all profit is paid out every year. Most companies will keep some back for a reserve (**unappropriated profit**), and this could be used, for example, to replace worn-out machinery. Sometimes profits may also be kept back to pay shareholders a dividend in another year when profits are expected to be poor.

DEBENTURES

A company can raise finance over and above selling shares by selling (issuing) **debentures**. A debenture is a loan to the company, and debenture holders are in no way shareholders. They have no vote or say in the running of the company. They are secured creditors, which means if the company goes bust they may seize assets from the company and sell them to get their money back. Debentures carry an annual fixed rate of interest which must be paid before any dividend is given to shareholders. At the end of the loan period, the value of the debenture must be repaid in full.

ONLINE

Head to www.brightredbooks.net for some extension material on debentures.

ONLINE TEST

Test yourself on preparing financial accounting information online at www.brightredbooks.net

 ## THINGS TO DO AND THINK ABOUT

Specimen exam-style questions:

1. Describe the main differences between a preference share and an ordinary share.
2. Explain what is meant by the stewardship function.
3. Describe three characteristics of a public limited company.
4. Explain the meaning of a share premium.
5. Describe three characteristics of a private limited company.
6. Outline one reason why a company may retain some profit within the business.
7. Describe what is meant by a debenture.

SETTING UP A LIMITED COMPANY

LEGAL DOCUMENTATION

As a limited company has a separate legal identity, there are several formal steps that must be taken in its formation. The two major controlling documents of a company are its Memorandum of Association and its Articles of Association.

Memorandum of Association

This is a document signed by the first members of the company, setting out the company's constitution and its powers. It governs the relationship of the company with the outside world and contains six main clauses:

1. the name of the company, ending with the words 'public limited company' in the case of public companies or with the word 'limited' in the case of private companies (the Memorandum of a public company will state that it is to be a public limited company)
2. a statement as to whether the registered office of the company is to be in England, Wales or Scotland
3. an outline of the objectives of the company (the aims the company will pursue)
4. a statement that the liability of the members is limited to the value of the shares purchased
5. the amount of share equity with which the company proposes to be registered, and its division into shares of a fixed amount
6. the association clause, which is an undertaking signed by the founder members of the company, stating that they wish to form a company and that each agrees to purchase the number of shares specified against his/her name.

Articles of Association

These are regulations for the internal management of the company. They define the method of appointment and duties of the directors and company secretary, the directors' borrowing powers, the provisions about notice of general meetings and the procedure to be followed at such meetings, regulations concerning the issue of shares and their transfer, voting rights of shareholders and the provision as to audits, accounts and so on.

These regulations are of the utmost importance when it is realised that the legal owners of the business, the shareholders, have entrusted the running of the company to the directors.

The Companies Act 1989

This Act makes the keeping of proper sets of accounting records and the preparation of financial statements compulsory for every company. In addition, the accounts must be audited, this being quite different from a partnership or sole trader's business, where an audit is not compulsory at all. The Act also lays down the format for the Income Statement and the Statement of Financial Position.

Annual report

At least once every year, UK companies are required to present to their shareholders information about their financial results in the form of an annual report.

Information which is required by law includes:

1. Notice of AGM and agenda
2. Directors' report
3. Income Statement and Statement of Financial Position
4. Notes to accounts
5. Statement of accounting policies
6. Auditors' report.

INTANGIBLE ASSETS OF A COMPANY

Preliminary expenses

When a company is formed, it is obliged to meet certain preliminary (or formation) expenses, for example legal expenses. It may also need to publish a prospectus if it is a public limited company which is appealing to the public for share equity. These preliminary expenses are quite unavoidable, yet they result in little more than a certificate of incorporation, which is like the 'birth certificate' of a company, and a certificate of trading, which permits the company to commence trading. Several thousand pounds may have been spent, yet the only **assets** obtained are these two documents. Preliminary expenses are considered to be **intangible non-current assets** and are normally written out of the Statement of Financial Position within a few years of trading.

Goodwill

Goodwill is also an intangible asset and is usually based on the reputation and connections which has been built up by the firm in the past. It is most likely to arise as an accounting entry if one firm acquires another firm, and the purchase price exceeds the value of the assets acquired – the excess is regarded as being for the asset of goodwill. One company may be influenced into paying more than just the asset value for another company because of:

1. the location of the company acquired
2. the personal reputation of the company acquired
3. good workforce and management
4. the profit record of the company acquired
5. possession of trademarks and patents
6. retention of favourable contracts with suppliers/customers.

Even though goodwill is listed as an asset, it cannot be bought or sold. As such, many accountants and analysts prefer not to consider it when they are examining a firm's accounts. The real value of goodwill depends on future possibilities, not past happenings. Thus it follows that it is usually prudent to write it down as quickly as possible after its introduction into the books, for the future is uncertain. *This involves goodwill being written down in the appropriation section of the Income Statement and a reduction of goodwill in the non-current assets section in the Statement of Financial Position.*

Investments

It is often the case that one company will invest in another company in the hope of earning additional revenue. Shares purchased in another company are likely to earn dividends annually. The investment itself is an intangible asset and will also appear in the non-current assets section of the Statement of Financial Position. Any annual return on the investment will be recorded in the Income Statement under 'other income'.

THINGS TO DO AND THINK ABOUT

Specimen exam-style questions:

1. **Describe** the essential information that would be recorded in a company's Memorandum of Association.
2. **Explain** the purpose of a company's Articles of Association.
3. **Explain** why preliminary expenses and goodwill are recorded as intangible assets in a Statement of Financial Position.

DON'T FORGET

Preliminary expenses are **intangible assets** and **not** business expenses!

DON'T FORGET

Goodwill is an intangible asset and is listed in the non-current assets section in the Statement of Financial Position.

ONLINE

Head to www.brightredbooks. net for exercises on company accounts.

ONLINE TEST

Test yourself on preparing financial accounting information online at www.brightredbooks.net

FINAL ACCOUNTS OF A PUBLIC LIMITED COMPANY

Now that you know about the accounts that plcs are legally required to submit, let's have a look at this example of the final accounts for 'Accounting plc'.

Example:

Accounting plc
Income Statement for the year ended 31 December Year 2

	£000s	£000s	£000s
Sales revenue (1)			522
Less sales returns (2)			50
Net sales revenue (3)			472
Less cost of sales			
Opening inventory (4)		30	
Add purchases (5)	400		
Carriage in (6)	20		
	420		
Less purchases returns (7)	25	415	
		415	
Closing inventory (8)		55	
		360	
Warehouse expenses (9)		20	
COST OF SALES			380
Gross profit (10)			92
Less expenses (11)			
Office expenses		18	
Selling expenses		27	
Bad debts		3	
Loan finance cost		2	
Debenture finance cost		4	
Provision for depreciation – equipment		5	59
			33
Add other income (12)			
Dividends due on investments		5	
Decrease in provision for bad debts		2	7
PROFIT FOR THE YEAR BEFORE TAX			40
Less corporation tax (25%) (13)			10
PROFIT FOR THE YEAR AFTER TAX			30
Add unappropriated profit at 1 January (14)			53
			83
Less (15)			
Preference dividend		10	
Ordinary dividend		3	
Goodwill written down		20	33
UNAPPROPRIATED PROFIT at 31 December (16)			50

No.	Terminology	Meaning
1	Sales revenue	Money the business receives from customers from selling their goods or services.
2	Sales returns	Total value of goods returned to the business from customers, for example because the goods sold were faulty.
3	Net sales revenue	Sales revenue – Sales returns = Net sales revenue
4	Opening inventory	Inventory (closing inventory) from the previous accounting period. This will normally be the first inventory sold during the current accounting period.
5	Purchases	Total value of inventory purchased from suppliers by the business for resale.
6	Carriage in	A charge added to purchases when the supplier delivers inventory to the business's premises. It is sometimes referred to as a delivery charge.
7	Purchases returns	Total value of inventory returned to suppliers by the business, for example where the wrong goods were delivered by the supplier or where a greater quantity than was ordered was delivered.
8	Closing inventory	Inventory unsold at the end of an accounting period. This will also appear as a current asset in the Statement of Financial Position and is likely to be sold in the next accounting period.
9	Warehouse expenses	The costs incurred in storing inventory in a warehouse prior to sale.
10	Gross profit	This is the result of subtracting the cost of sales from net sales revenue.
11	Expenses	All expenses of running the business for the year are listed, totalled and deducted from gross profit. Note: expenses will be adjusted to show what should have been paid and not what actually was paid.
12	Other income	These are other items of income the business has received during the accounting year from sources other than buying and selling goods.
13	Corporation tax	A plc is required by law to pay corporation tax on its annual profits. The amount is deducted from profit for the year before tax. The rate of corporation tax is set by the Chancellor of the Exchequer in his/her annual budget.
14	Unappropriated profit at start	Retained profits (profits not distributed) from the previous accounting period. These increase the available profit to the business for the current year.
15	Distribution of profits	A breakdown of how the current year's profits are to be used/distributed. For example, any dividend paid to shareholders is shown in this section.
16	Unappropriated profit at end	Profit from the current year that will be retained in the business for use in the future. Unappropriated profit will be shown as a reserve in the Statement of Financial Position.

DON'T FORGET

All accounting statements must show the name of the business and the statement being prepared.

DON'T FORGET

All business expenses must be adjusted to take account of amounts owing and amounts prepaid.

contd

Accounting Plc
Statement of Financial Position as at 31 December Year 2

	£000s Cost	£000s Depreciation	£000s NBV
Non-current assets (1)			
Property	326	–60	386
Equipment	25	2	23
Intangible assets (2)			
Goodwill			50
Preliminary expenses			10
			469
Current assets (3)			
Closing inventory		55	
Trade receivables		39	
Electricity receivable		4	
		98	
Current liabilities (4)			
Trade payables	8		
Cash and cash equivalents	9		
Wages payable	8	25	
Working equity (5)			73
Net assets employed (6)			542
Non-current liabilities (7)			
4% debentures		100	
Bank loan		20	120
Net assets			422
Equity (8)			
100,000 £1 ordinary shares		100	
200,000 £1 5% preference shares		200	300
Reserves (9)			
Revaluation reserve		60	
Share premium (10)		12	
Unappropriated profit		50	122
			422

 **DON'T FORGET**

Amounts paid in advance during a financial period are recorded as **current assets** in the Statement of Financial Position.

 **DON'T FORGET**

Amounts still owing at the end of a financial period are recorded as **current liabilities** in the Statement of Financial Position.

ONLINE

Find exercises on company accounts at www.brightredbooks.net

No.	Terminology	Meaning
1	**Non-current assets**	Items owned by the business, and which will remain in the business for a long period – more than one year. These assets are not primarily purchased for resale. Usually the business cannot function without these assets. Non-current assets are reduced in value over time to take account of depreciation.
2	**Intangible assets**	These are assets of a business that are not physical in nature. You can see and touch tangible assets such as machinery or equipment, but you cannot see or touch goodwill. Preliminary expenses are also an example of an intangible asset.
3	**Current assets**	These are assets owned by the business which will be kept for less than one year. Their value changes from day to day. These assets are primarily for conversion into cash.
4	**Current liabilities**	Those liabilities (debts) which are usually paid within one year, for example trade payables for goods purchased.
5	**Working equity**	This is simply the difference between current assets and current liabilities.
6	**Net assets employed**	Net assets employed = Non-current assets + Working equity.
7	**Non-current liabilities**	Long-term debts to the business that will take more than one year to pay off. Large bank loans and mortgages will be repaid over a number of years.
8	**Equity**	The money provided by the owner(s) of the business to start and run it.
9	**Reserves**	Amounts set aside out of profits for particular purposes, such as to equalise dividends over the years or to replace equipment when it wears out. These are known as revenue reserves.
		Reserves may also arise out of revaluation of non-current assets. For example, if property increases in value, this will be recorded in the non-current assets section of the Statement of Financial Position. The increase on revaluation will also be recorded as a capital reserve in the equity section of the Statement of Financial Position.
10	**Share premium**	This is the difference between the selling price and the face value of shares. It is important to note that share premium only arises when the company is able to sell shares above their face value. Share premium is a reserve and is usually used to issue bonus shares to shareholders.

THINGS TO DO AND THINK ABOUT

1. Explain the difference between gross profit and profit for the year.

2. Explain what is meant by the term 'share premium'.

 ONLINE TEST

Test yourself on preparing financial accounting information online at www.brightredbooks.net

EXERCISES ON COMPANY ACCOUNTS

EXERCISE 1

The following trial balance was extracted from the books of Shubunkin Ltd at 31 December Year 2 after the preparation of the Income Statement.

	£	£
Authorised and issued share equity (80,000 shares) EQ		80,000
Share premium EQ		10,000
6% debentures LTL		20,000
Freehold property (at cost) NCA	70,000	
Furniture and fittings (at cost) NCA	4,000	
Inventory in trade at end of year CA	28,950	
Wages and salaries due		350
Provision for bad debts, 1 January Year 2 TR		400
Provision for depreciation – furniture and fittings AGG DEP		1,200
Trade receivables CA	15,000 ~400	
Trade payables CL		9,280
Cash and cash equivalents CA	19,200	
Debenture interest due CL		600
Rates in advance CA	50	
Interim dividend paid APP	8,000	
Unappropriated profit at 1 January Year 2 APP		3,300
Profit for year		20,070
	145,200	145,200

Prepare the appropriation section of the Income Statement for the year 31 December Year 2 and a Statement of Financial Position as at that date.

EXERCISE 2

The following trial balance was extracted from the books of Rostrevor Ltd on 31 December Year 2.

	£	£
Equity (authorised and issued) 80,000 ordinary shares EQ		80,000
20,000 preference shares (7%) EQ		20,000
Motor vans at cost NCA	14,460	
Freehold property (at cost) NCA	95,200	
Premium on preference shares EQ (SP)		2,000
Provision for depreciation – motor vans AGDP		10,142
Inventory in trade at 31 December Year 2 CA	17,754	
Provision for bad debts at 31 December Year 2		400
Unappropriated profit at 1 January Year 2 APP		10,680
Cash and cash equivalents CA	4,770	
Trade receivables and trade payables	CA 28,325 ~400	CL 24,150
Rates and insurance in advance CA	272	
Wages due CL		944
Ordinary dividend paid APP	8,000	
Preference dividend paid APP	1,400	
Profit for year		21,865
	170,181	170,181

Prepare the appropriation section of the Income Statement for the year 31 December Year 2 and a Statement of Financial Position as at that date.

EXERCISE 3

From the following trial balance of Andrews plc, prepare the final accounts for the year ended 31 December Year 2.

contd

	£	£
Share equity (authorised and issued) 200,000 ordinary shares EQ		200,000
6% debentures LTL		40,000
Property at cost N CA	265,000	
Fixtures and fittings at cost NCA	12,000	
Trade receivables CA	18,950 -300	
Trade payables CL		12,930
Intangible assets (preliminary expenses) APP	2,000	
Opening inventory T	18,930	
Provision for bad debts £		300
Debenture interest to 30 June Year 2 PRL (6%x40000)	1,200 CL	
Provision for depreciation – fixtures and fittings A GG DEP		6,000
Cash and cash equivalents CL		24,490
Wages and salaries PRL	23,360	
Rent and rates RL	1,650	
Other operating expenses PRL	5,120	
Bad debts PRL	1,510	
Unappropriated profit at 1 January Year 2 APP		14,740
Purchases T	164,740	
Ordinary dividend paid APP	24,000	
Sales revenue T		240,000
	538,460	538,460

You are given the following information:

1. Inventory at 31 December Year 2 is £20,470.
2. The provision for bad debts is to be increased to £350.
3. Depreciation at 5% per annum on cost is to be charged on fixtures and fittings.
4. Rates paid in advance are £75.
5. Wages outstanding are £240.
6. One fifth of the preliminary expenses is to be written off in the appropriation account.
7. The outstanding debenture interest is to be paid.

 EXERCISE 4

Solarheaters Ltd has an authorised equity of £80,000 divided into 160,000 ordinary shares of £0.50 each.

The following balances were extracted from the books at 31 December Year 2.

	£
Issued equity (fully paid)	50,000
Unappropriated profit at 1 January Year 2	1,260
Profit for the year to 31 December Year 2	35,270
Fixtures and fittings at cost	6,000
Machinery at cost	35,800
Provision for depreciation – fixtures and fittings	1,200
Provision for depreciation – machinery	4,900
Freehold property at cost	38,400
Inventory	9,900
Trade receivables	8,200
Provision for bad debts	550
Trade payables	3,260
Cash and cash equivalents (Cr)	6,860
Ordinary dividend paid	5,000

Prepare the appropriation section of the Income Statement for year ending 31 December Year 2.

 THINGS TO DO AND THINK ABOUT

1. Describe, using examples, what is meant by non-current assets.
2. Explain why rates and insurance in advance is a current asset.
3. Explain the difference between trade receivables and trade payables.
4. Describe what is meant by preliminary expenses.
5. Explain the difference between authorised and issued share equity.
6. Explain the difference between a private limited company and a public limited company.

ADJUSTMENTS IN FINAL ACCOUNTS: METHODS OF DEPRECIATION

There are four key adjustments that are usually required to be accounted for when preparing the final accounts (Income Statement and Statement of Financial Position) of a business organisation. These four adjustments are:

1. depreciation of non-current assets
2. bad debts/provision for doubtful debts – trade receivables who are unable/unwilling to pay
3. amounts paid in advance at the end of an accounting period
4. amounts still owing at the end of the accounting period.

The accounting treatment of these four areas will be exactly the same whether the business is a sole trader, partnership, limited company or manufacturing business.

DEPRECIATION OF NON-CURRENT ASSETS

Non-current assets have been defined as long-term assets, high in value, owned by the business for use in the business. Most non-current assets have a limited useful life and fall in value over time. This fall in value of non-current assets is called **depreciation**. Depreciation of non-current assets occurs for a number of reasons. These reasons include:

- **Use** – as an asset is used, its value decreases.
- **Wear and tear** – use of machinery or vehicles, or exposure to bad weather.
- **Time** – with the passage of time, the asset decreases in value.
- **Obsolescence** – changes in technology often mean that more sophisticated and efficient non-current assets become available.

As a non-current asset loses value, its value must be decreased in the accounting records of the business by writing off the reduction to a **provision for depreciation account**.

Note: the only non-current asset that does not depreciate in value is land, since this has an infinite life.

Methods of depreciation

There are two main methods of calculating depreciation: **straight line** and **diminishing balance**.

DON'T FORGET

Adjustments to final accounts affect all types of businesses – sole traders, partnerships, companies and manufacturing companies.

DON'T FORGET

The fall in value of non-current assets is referred to as depreciation.

DON'T FORGET

There are two main methods of calculating depreciation - **straight line** and **diminishing balance**.

VIDEO LINK

For an overview of these methods of depreciation, go online and watch the video at www.brightredbooks.net

Example:

Grants Ltd decide to depreciate their motor van by £2,000 per year due to use. Here are the ledger accounts at the end of year 1:

Motor van a/c

Date	Details	Dr	Cr	Balance
1 Jan 20..	Balance	10,000		10,000 (Dr)

Provision for depreciation a/c

Date	Details	Dr	Cr	Balance
31 Dec 20..	Income Statement		2,000	2,000 (Cr)

At the end of the accounting year, the £2,000 will then be **debited** (charged) to the Income Statement as an expense.

STRAIGHT-LINE METHOD

The straight-line method of depreciation is where the same amount of depreciation is written off the non-current asset each year. To calculate the depreciation to be charged annually, the accountant will deduct the scrap value of the asset from the cost of the asset and divide the result by the estimated life of the asset.

Formula:

$$\text{Annual depreciation} = \frac{\text{Cost of non-current asset} - \text{Scrap value}}{\text{Estimated life of non-current asset}}$$

DIMINISHING-BALANCE METHOD

By this method, a fixed percentage for depreciation is deducted from the cost of the non-current asset in the first year. In the second or later years, the same percentage is taken off the reduced/diminished balance (i.e. cost *less* depreciation already charged). This method is also known as the **reducing-balance method**.

Example:

If a machine is bought for £10,000, and depreciation is to be charged at 20%, the calculations for the first three years would be:

Cost	£10,000
Depreciation Year 1 (20%)	2,000
Reduced balance	8,000
Depreciation Year 2	
(20% of £8,000)	1,600
Reduced balance	6,400
Depreciation Year 3	
(20% of £6,400)	1,280
Reduced balance	5,120

Straight-line method		Diminishing-balance method	
Advantages	Disadvantages	Advantages	Disadvantages
• It is straightforward and fairly easy to calculate. • It is simple to understand. • The non-current asset is written off over a definite period of time to its predicted scrap value.	• When a new non-current asset is purchased or an existing non-current asset is sold, depreciation has to be recalculated. • The charge to the Income Statement increases over the years because of increased repair and maintenance costs. • There is no provision for replacement of the asset at the end of its useful life.	• It is easy to calculate, and recalculations are not necessary with purchase or sale of a non-current asset. • The charge against profits is more evenly spread over the life of the asset, since the diminishing charge for depreciation is offset against increased charges for repairs. • It clearly highlights that, for most non-current assets, the annual loss in value is greatest in the early years of the asset's working life.	• It is more difficult to calculate compared with the straight-line method. • It is not a good method for assets with a short working life. • There is no provision for the replacement of the non-current asset.

DEPRECIATION AND THE INCOME STATEMENT AND THE STATEMENT OF FINANCIAL POSITION

These two extracts show how depreciation would appear in the Income Statement and the Statement of Financial Position.

Extract 1 – Income Statement

	£	£
Gross profit		44,000
Less expenses		
Rent and rates	1,400	
Heat and light	1,200	
Wages and salaries		8,200
Discount allowed	2,500	
Loan interest	1,600	
Van depreciation	2,000	16,900
		27,100

Extract 2 – Statement of Financial Position

	£	£	£
Non-current assets	Cost	Depreciation	NBV
Property	50,000	–	50,000
Motor van	12,000	2,000	10,000

Depreciation is an expense to the business. Non-current assets can also be shown at cost (how much the business paid for the assets when they were purchased new), the accumulated depreciation to date and the net book value (NBV) in the non-current assets section of the Statement of Financial Position.

THINGS TO DO AND THINK ABOUT

Prepare a short PowerPoint presentation for your class to cover:

- the definition of depreciation
- the straight-line method of calculating depreciation
- the reducing-balance method of calculating depreciation
- the advantages and disadvantages of each method of calculating depreciation.

DON'T FORGET

Straight-line method – the same amount of depreciation is charged each year.

ONLINE

Head to www.brightredbooks.net for exercises on calculating depreciation using the straight-line method.

DON'T FORGET

Reducing-balance method: a fixed percentage is used to calculate the annual rate of depreciation. The charge for depreciation reduces each year.

ONLINE

Head to www.brightredbooks.net for exercises on calculating depreciation using the diminishing-balance method.

DON'T FORGET

Depreciation is an expense in the Income Statement. Non-current assets must be reduced by the aggregate depreciation in the Statement of Financial Position.

ONLINE TEST

Head to www.brightredbooks.net to test yourself on adjustments.

ONLINE

Find short-answer questions on this topic at www.brightredbooks.net

ADJUSTMENTS IN FINAL ACCOUNTS: AMOUNTS PAID IN ADVANCE/OWING

AMOUNTS PAID IN ADVANCE

This is where the business has **paid more** than it should have for the accounting period, and so the amount actually paid has to be **reduced** in order to show what should have been paid. For example, if the business **paid £400** for telephone bills, but the actual telephone bill for the accounting year was **£300**, then the business has **paid £100 in advance**.

The figure which would be charged to the Income Statement would be **£300** (the actual cost of the telephone bill), and **£100** would appear as 'other receivables (telephone)' in the **current assets** section of the business's Statement of Financial Position.

Extracts 3 and 4 below show how payments in advance would appear in the Income Statement and the Statement of Financial Position.

DON'T FORGET

Amounts paid in advance are current assets in the Statement of Financial Position.

Extract 3 – Income Statement

	£	£
Gross profit		24,000
Less expenses		
Telephone (£400 – £100)	300	
Heat and light	1,100	
Wages and salaries	6,500	
Discount allowed	1,400	
Loan interest	800	
Van depreciation	2,000	12,100
		11,900

Extract 4 – Statement of Financial Position

Current assets

Inventory	4,800
Trade receivables	6,200
Cash and cash equivalents	8,500
Other receivables (telephone)	100

Sometimes there will be expenses paid in advance at both the start and end of a financial year. Look at the example shown below.

Example:

At the start of Year 2, £100 had been prepaid for telephone. £600 is paid during Year 2, and of that £600 paid, £200 was for Year 3. Year 2 telephone expense would be calculated as follows:

Telephone prepaid at start of Year 2	£100
Telephone paid during Year 2	£600
	£700
Telephone prepaid at end of Year 2	£200
Actual telephone expense for Year 2	£500

 **EXERCISE 1**

From the information alongside, prepare the expenses section of the Income Statement of S. Grant for the year ended 31 December Year 2.

Gross profit £45,000

Expense	Paid during Year 2	Paid in advance at start of Year 2	Paid in advance at end of Year 2
Rent	£5,000	£200	£300
Salaries	£12,000	£2,000	£600
Insurance	£1,400	£80	£120
Telephone	£400	£50	£20
Electricity	£900	£250	£300

EXERCISE 2

From the information alongside, prepare the expenses section of the Income Statement of C. McKay for the year ended 31 December Year 2.

Gross profit £60,000

Expense	Paid during Year 2	Paid in advance at start of Year 2	Paid in advance at end of Year 2
Salaries	£21,000	£2,000	£3,500
Electricity	£1,500	£100	£225
Cleaning	£2,500	£50	£75
Telephone	£700	£40	£32
Insurance	£850	£25	£75

contd

AMOUNTS OWING

This is where the business has **amounts owing** at the end of the accounting period, and so the amount actually paid has to **be increased** in order to show what **should have been paid**. For example, if the business **paid £200** for cleaning expenses, but the actual cleaning expenses for the accounting year were **£400**, then the business has **expenses owing** of **£200**.

The figure which would be charged to the Income Statement would be **£400** (the actual cost of the cleaning expenses), and **£200** would appear as other payables (cleaning expenses) in the **current liabilities** section of the Statement of Financial Position.

Extracts 5 and 6 below show how amounts owing would appear in the Income Statement and the Statement of Financial Position.

Extract 5 – Income Statement

	£	£
Gross profit		35,000
Less expenses		
Telephone	300	
Heat and light	1,400	
Wages and salaries	10,500	
Discount allowed	1,200	
Cleaning expenses		
(£200 + £200)	400	
Van depreciation	2,000	15,800
		19,200

Extract 6 – Statement of Financial Position
Current liabilities

Trade payables	2,600
Value-added tax	1,500
Other payables (cleaning expenses)	200

DON'T FORGET

Amounts owing at the end of an accounting period are recorded as **current liabilities** in the Statement of Financial Position.

ONLINE

You can find the answers to all of the exercises in this book, as well as a wealth of extra activities, at www.brightredbooks.net

 **EXERCISE 3**

During the financial year ending 31 December Year 2, Young and Grant made the following payments:

Salaries	£12,600
Insurance	£8,200
Rent	£14,500
Telephone	£650
Salaries	£12,000
Electricity	£1,340
Discounts allowed	£80
Depreciation	£500

At the end of Year 2, the following amounts were due to be paid:

Salaries	£600
Insurance	£120
Rent	£500
Telephone	£125

Gross profit for the year was £85,000.

You are required to prepare the expenses section of the Income Statement for Year 2 to calculate profit for the year.

ONLINE TEST

Head to www.brightredbooks.net to test yourself on adjustments.

 **EXERCISE 4**

From the information alongside, prepare the expenses section of the Income Statement of Henderson's Ltd for the year ended 31 December Year 1.

Gross profit for Year 1 was £82,000.

Expense	Amount paid during Year 1	Amount owing at the end of Year 1
Rent	£12,200	£1,800
Insurance	£1,500	£100
Cleaning expenses	£800	
Salaries	£25,400	£1,400
Telephone	£400	£75
Electricity	£2,600	£80

 THINGS TO DO AND THINK ABOUT

Answer the following questions in your workbook.

1. List four business expenses that could be subject to over- or underpayment at the end of an accounting period.

2. Explain how payments in advance at the end of an accounting period are recorded in the final accounts of a public limited company.

3. Using an example, explain how amounts owing at the end of an accounting period are recorded in the final accounts of a private limited company.

BAD DEBTS/PROVISION FOR DOUBTFUL DEBTS

Bad debts/provision for doubtful debts refers to trade receivables (debtors) unable/unwilling to pay.

BAD DEBTS

There will be occasions when trade receivables are unwilling or unable to pay what is owing to the business. It could be the case that the customer disputes the amount owing, or perhaps they have been declared bankrupt. These debts will be written off in the customer's personal account and will therefore be an expense in the profit and loss section of the business's Income Statement. This is shown in extract 7 here.

If we fail to write off a debt that we know is not going to be recovered, the effect will be to overstate profit by the amount of the bad debt.

Extract 7 – Income Statement

	£	£
Gross profit		32,000
Less expenses		
Bad debts	620	
Telephone	400	
Heat and light	1,500	
Wages and salaries	8,200	
Discount allowed	900	
Cleaning expenses (£200 + £200)	400	
Van depreciation	2,000	14,020
		17,980

PROVISION FOR DOUBTFUL DEBTS

Following the prudence concept, some business organisations may also decide to create a provision for trade receivables (debtors) who **might** not pay.

The 'provision for doubtful debts' figure is usually calculated as a percentage of the total trade receivables at the end of the financial year.

In the **first year** of trading, the total provision for doubtful debts is written off in the profit-and-loss section of the Income Statement.

However, in subsequent years the difference between last year's figure and the current year's figure is written off to the profit and loss section of the Income Statement.

The provision for doubtful debts will also be deducted from trade receivables in the Statement of Financial Position to ensure a true and fair view of the business. This is shown in extracts 8 and 9 below.

Extract 8 – Income Statement

	£	£
Gross profit		29,000
Less expenses		
Bad debts	620	
Provision for doubtful debts	500	
Telephone	700	
Heat and light	1,850	
Wages and salaries	6,100	
Discount allowed	200	
Cleaning expenses (£200 + £200)	400	
Van depreciation	2,000	12,370
		16,630

Extract 9 – Statement of Financial Position

Current assets	
Inventory	4,800
Trade receivables (£5,000 – £500)	4,500
Cash and cash equivalents	8,500
Other receivables (telephone)	100

The provision for doubtful debts for subsequent years may be more or less than the previous year. If the new provision is **less than** the previous year, then a reduction in provision for doubtful debts will be recorded under 'Other income' and will increase profits. However, if the figure is **more than** the previous year, the difference will be recorded as an increase in the provision for doubtful debts in the expenses section of the Income Statement. This is shown in examples 1 and 2 below.

contd

DON'T FORGET

Bad debts are written off as an expense in the Income Statement.

DON'T FORGET

Accounting statements must give a true and fair view of a business.

DON'T FORGET

Accountants should be prudent and never overstate profits.

DON'T FORGET

Doubtful debts are trade receivables who are unlikely to pay.

DON'T FORGET

A decrease in provision for doubtful debts is a gain and increases profits. An increase in provision for doubtful debts is an expense and reduces profits.

Example 1:

Assume the provision for doubtful debts was £500 in Year 1. If the provision for doubtful debts is anticipated to be £550 (increase of £50) in Year 2, the entries in the Income Statement and Statement of Financial Position in Year 2 would be as follows:

Income Statement

	£	£
Gross profit		21,000
Less expenses		
Bad debts	620	
Increase in provision for doubtful debts	50	
Telephone	520	
Heat and light	780	
Wages and salaries	9,200	
Discount allowed	300	
Cleaning expenses (£200 + £200)	400	
Van depreciation	2,000	13,870
		7,130

Statement of Financial Position
Current assets

Inventory	2,600	
Trade receivables (£5,500 – £550)	4,950	
Cash and cash equivalents	4,500	
Other receivables (electricity)	200	

Example 2:

Assume the provision for doubtful debts was £500 in Year 1. If the provision for doubtful debts is anticipated to be £450 (decrease of £50) in Year 2, the entries in the Income Statement and Statement of Financial Position for Year 2 would be as follows:

Income Statement

	£	£
Gross profit		21,000
Less expenses		
Bad debts	620	
Telephone	520	
Heat and light	780	
Wages and salaries	9,200	
Discount allowed	300	
Cleaning expenses (£200 + £200)	400	
Van depreciation	2,000	13,870
		7,130
Add other income		
Rent received	500	
Reduction in provision for doubtful debts	50	
Profit for the year		7,680

Statement of Financial Position
Current assets

Inventory	2,600	
Trade receivables (£5,500 – £450)	5,050	
Cash and cash equivalents	4,500	
Other receivables (electricity)	200	

The following table summarises the procedures for dealing with increases and decreases in the provision for doubtful debts:

Increase in provision for doubtful debts	1. Calculate the new provision for doubtful debts 2. Calculate **increase in provision** (new provision less previous provision) 3. Record **increase in provision** in the expenses section of the Income Statement 4. Deduct entire new provision from trade receivables in the Statement of Financial Position.
Decrease in provision for doubtful debts	1. Calculate new provision for doubtful debts 2. Calculate **decrease in provision** (previous provision less new provision) 3. Record **decrease in provision** in the **Other Income** section of the Income Statement (i.e. add back to gross profit) 4. Deduct entire new provision from trade receivables in the Statement of Financial Position.

EXERCISE 1

The following figures have been taken from the accounts of Grants Ltd on 31 December:

Trade receivables (Year 2)	£10,000
Provision for doubtful debts (Year 1)	£400
Bad debts (Year 2)	£250

In Year 2, the provision for doubtful debts is to be 8% of trade receivables.

You are required to:

1. calculate the increase or decrease in provision for doubtful debts in Year 2
2. calculate net trade receivables to be shown in the Statement of Financial Position as at 31 December Year 2.

VIDEO LINK

For an overview of increases and decreases in the provision for doubtful debts, go online and watch the video at www.brightredbooks.net

ONLINE

Find further exercises on bad debts at www.brightredbooks.net

ONLINE TEST

Head to www.brightredbooks.net to test yourself on bad debts.

THINGS TO DO AND THINK ABOUT

Answer the following questions in sentences in your workbook.

1. Explain what is meant by a bad debt.
2. Outline one reason why a trade receivable may be unable to pay.
3. State how bad debts are recorded in the final accounts of a business organisation.
4. Explain one reason why it is important that bad debts are written off.
5. Explain what is meant by a provision for doubtful debts.
6. Explain how an increase in the provision for doubtful debts is recorded in the final accounts of a business.
7. Explain how a decrease in the provision for doubtful debts is recorded in the final accounts of a business.

COMPANY ACCOUNTS: EXAM-STYLE EXERCISES

⚙ EXERCISE 1

The following Trial Balance was extracted from the books of Lowland Enterprises Ltd at 31 March Year 2.

	£	£
Issued and fully paid share equity EQ + 75000		100,000
6% debentures NCL		50,000
Trade payables CL		8,000
Unappropriated profit at 1 April Year 2 APP		28,000
Cash and cash equivalents CL		18,000
Property at cost NCA	100,000	
Inventory at 1 April Year 2 T	10,000	
Trade receivables CA	30,000	
Sales T		198,000
Share premium R + EQ	−25000 32,000	
Goodwill NCA	60,000 −10000	
Debenture interest P&L	3,000	
Plant: cost NCA	80,000	
Delivery vans: cost NCA	20,000	
Provision for depreciation at 1 April Year 2		
Plant ⎱ AGG DEP	+8000 40,000	
Vans ⎰	+3000 10,000	
Purchases T	33,000	
Wages P&L	65,000+1500	
Expenses P&L	45,000	
Administration expenses P&L	10,000	
Selling and delivery expenses P&L	20,000 −3000+500	
Ordinary dividend paid APP	8,000	
	484,000	484,000

Notes:

1. Authorised share capital 150,000 shares of £1 each. EQ
2. Inventory at 31 March Year 2: £15,000. T& CA
3. Selling expenses include £3,000 prepaid. CA
4. Advertising leaflets, cost £500, were awaiting collection from the printers on 31 March Year 2. The invoice for this item, dated 16 March Year 2, has not yet been CL passed through the accounts of Lowland Enterprises Ltd.
5. Wages due and unpaid at 31 March Year 2 were £1,500. CL
6. Depreciate fixed assets using the straight-line method as follows: plant 10%; vans 15%. P&L
    8R   3R

7. The directors intend to use the balance on the share premium account to make an issue of 1 bonus share for every 4 shares held.
8. Write down goodwill by £10,000. APP

You are required to prepare the Income Statement for the year ended 31 December Year 2 and a Statement of Financial Position as at that date.

⚙ EXERCISE 2

The following balances were taken from the ledger of Craigmore Ltd on 31 March Year 2.

	Dr £000s	Cr £000s
750,000 ordinary shares of £1 each EQ		750
250,000 8% preference shares of £1 each EQ		250
10% debentures NCL		200
Unappropriated profit at 1 April Year 2 APP		137
Sales revenue T		2,377
Purchases T	1,278	
Inventory at 1 April Year 2 T	160	
Wages P&L	434	
Insurance P&L	45	
Carriage in T	5	
Carriage out P&L	4	
Rent ⎱ P&L	30	
Bad debts ⎰	47	
Discount received 0 I		12
Debenture interest P&L	10+10(CL)	
Dividend on ordinary shares APP	40	
Machinery at cost NCA	1,130	
Vehicles at cost	550 − 90 ×75%	
Trade receivables CA	155 − 9	
Trade payables CL		109
Investments (long-term) NCA (ITA)	200	
VAT CL		13
Cash and cash equivalents CA	67 −20	
Provisions for depreciation at 1 April Year 2		
Machinery ⎱ AGG DEP		+113 214
Vehicles ⎰		+115 90
Provision for doubtful debts at 1 April Year 2		3
	4,155	4,155

contd

Notes:

1. On 31 March Year 2, dividends of £8,000 on the long-term investments were owing to Craigmore Ltd. *Ōt + CA*

2. Provide for depreciation for the year as follows: machinery at 10% on cost; vehicles at 25% on the diminishing balance. *P&L* *AGG DEP*

3. Inventory at 31 March Year 2 was valued at £76,000. *T&CA*

4. On 31 March Year 2, rent owing amounted to £5,000, and insurance of £4,000 was prepaid. *CL* *CA*

5. The debentures were issued on 1 April Year 2. The final interest payment for the year has not yet been made.

6. The provision for doubtful debts at 31 March Year 2 is to be increased to £4,000. *P&L*

7. Provide for corporation tax on profits at 25%. *CL* *APP*

8. The preference dividend for the year has been paid, but no record has been made in the accounts.

You are required to prepare, from the trial balance and notes:

An Income Statement for the year ended 31 March Year 2, and a Statement of Financial Position as at that date.

⚙ EXERCISE 3

The following balances were extracted from the ledger of Taylors Ltd on 31 March Year 2.

	Dr £000s	Cr £000s
70,000 ordinary shares of £1 each *EQ*		70
10% debentures (Year 20) *NCL*		40
Share premium		20
Loan	10	
Unappropriated profit at 1 April Year 2 *APP*		31
Sales revenue *T*		180
Purchases *T*	80	
Inventory at 1 April Year 2 *T*	15	
Wages *P&L*	38	
Insurance *P&L*	10	
Advertising *P&L*	6	
Bad debts *P&L*	9	
Dividend on ordinary shares	9	
Debenture interest	2	
Discounts allowed and received	1	6
Carriage in	2	
Warehouse expenses	11	
Trade receivables	29	
Trade payables		25
Cash and cash equivalents	1	
Property at cost	50	
Equipment at cost	120	
Vehicles at cost	30	
Provisions for depreciation at 1 April Year 2		
Equipment		30
Vehicles		18
Provision for doubtful debts at 1 April Year 2		3
	£423	£423

Notes:

1. Provide for depreciation for the year as follows: equipment at 10% on cost; vehicles at 25% diminishing balance.

2. The provision for doubtful debts is to be reduced to £1,000.

3. Inventory on 31 March Year 2 was valued at £17,000.

4. On 31 March Year 2, the following items were prepaid or owing:

   • Insurance prepaid £1,000;

   • Debenture interest owing £2,000;

   • Loan interest owing £1,000;

   • Warehouse expenses owing £4,000.

5. Provide for corporation tax on profits at 25%.

6. The directors propose to use the share premium account to make a bonus issue of one ordinary share for every five held. No dividends will be issued on these shares.

You are required to prepare an Income Statement for the year ended 31 March Year 2 and a Statement of Financial Position as at that date.

ONLINE

Find more exercises like this online at www.brightredbooks.net

ONLINE TEST

Test yourself on company accounts at www.brightredbooks.net

PARTNERSHIP FINAL ACCOUNTS

PARTNERSHIP

A partnership is an organisation made up of between 2 and 20 partners and is governed by the Partnership Act of 1890. Some organisations such as solicitors and accountants can have more than 20 partners.

Partnerships also have unlimited liability, which means that the partners can be pursued for their personal possessions to pay any debts of the business. Even if one partner has nothing, the other partner(s) will be pursued in order to pay the debts.

If a partnership agreement is drawn up, it should cover the following:

Advantages	Disadvantages
● Easy to set up ● Owners have cover if they have to take time off for holidays or sickness ● New partners bring more expertise into the business ● New partners bring in more finance for expansion	● Unlimited liability ● Decision-making can be slowed down due to disagreements ● Partnership is dissolved if a partner leaves or dies ● Smaller companies can still have difficulty raising equity for expansion ● Profits need to be shared among more people ● Decisions made by one partner are binding on all partners

Partnerships

- the manner in which profits and losses are to be shared
- the amount of equity each partner is to contribute
- whether equity accounts are fixed or not
- the amount of interest payable on partners' equity
- the amount of drawings allowed by the partners
- the amount of interest charged to partners for drawings
- any partnership salaries to be paid.

The liability of each partner is unlimited unless they are a **limited partner**. A limited partner is someone who contributes equity but is not responsible for any debts of the business and can only lose the equity that they invested. It is important to note that not all partners can be limited partners; at least one partner must be a **general partner**.

Partnership accounts

In the ledger of a partnership, each partner's equity invested will be shown in an **equity account**. If the partnership has agreed that equity accounts are to remain fixed, then each will also have a **current account** to record movements in their equity such as drawings, interest on drawings, interest on equity, interest on loans, salaries and share of profits/losses.

The final accounts of a partnership are drawn up in the same way as any other company, with an Income Statement and Statement of Financial Position. However, the Income Statement will have an appropriation section after the 'profit for the year' figure to show how the profits are to be shared out. Furthermore, the Statement of Financial Position is exactly the same, except that the 'financed by' section at the end will show partners' current account balances as well as their equity-account balances.

Example:

Campbell and Morrison are in partnership sharing profits and losses in the ratio of 3:2 respectively. They both receive interest on equity of 10% and are charged 5% interest on drawings. Morrison also receives a salary of £10,000 per annum. Campbell has also lent the business £5,000 for which she receives interest of 6%.
The following information is also available:

	Equity invested	Drawings for the year
Campbell	£30,000	£8,000
Morrison	£20,000	£5,000

The profit for the year before taking any of the above into account amounted to £60,000.
The Income Statement would be prepared as normal and would end with an appropriation section as follows:

Campbell and Morrison:
Income Statement Appropriation Account

	£	£
Profit for the year		60,000
Add interest on drawings		
Campbell	400	
Morrison	250	650
		60,650
Less interest on equity		
Campbell	3,000	
Morrison	2,000	5,000
		55,650
Less salary – Morrison		10,000
Residual profit		£45,650
Share of profit		
Campbell	27,390	
Morrison	18,260	£45,650

The partners will each have an equity account and a current account in the ledger. However,

contd

the equity accounts remain fixed with the original equity invested, with any increases/decreases in equity being recorded in their current accounts as follows:

Equity account: Campbell

	Dr	Cr	Bal	
Balance		£30,000	£30,000	Cr

Current account: Campbell

	Dr	Cr	Bal	
Interest on equity		3,000	3,000	Cr
Share of profits		27,390	30,390	Cr
Interest on loan		300	30,690	Cr
Drawings	8,000		22,690	Cr
Interest on drawings	400		22,290	Cr

Equity account: Morrison

	Dr	Cr	Bal	
Balance		£30,000	£30,000	Cr

Current account: Morrison

	Dr	Cr	Bal	
Interest on equity		2,000	2,000	Cr
Salary		10,000	12,000	Cr
Share of profits		18,260	30,260	Cr
Drawings	5,000		25,260	Cr
Interest on drawings	250		25,010	Cr

Points to note

In the appropriation section, the business is charging the partners interest on their drawings, which means they are paying the business that money. This is why it is **added** to the profit for the year.

Interest on equity, salaries and share of profits are being paid by the business to the partners, which is why they are **deducted** from the profit for the year.

Interest on loans from the partners to the business is deducted in the expenses section of the Income Statement and credited to the current account.

The current account is an extension of the partner's equity account. For that reason, any money being paid to the partner from profits will add to their equity. As a result, interest on equity, interest on loan, salary and share of profits are credited. Any items which reduce the partner's equity are debited, i.e. drawings and interest on drawings.

Statement of Financial Position

Given that the current account forms part of the overall equity invested in the business by a partner, it is necessary to show these balances alongside the original equity balances in the 'financed by' section of the Statement of Financial Position.

Example:

Campbell and Morrison: Statement of Financial Position (Extract)
Financed by

	£	£
EQUITY		
Campbell	30,000	
Morrison	20,000	50,000
CURRENT ACCOUNTS		
Campbell	21,990	
Morrison	25,010	47,000
		£97,000

THINGS TO DO AND THINK ABOUT

1. Outline two advantages of forming a partnership rather than a sole trader.
2. State two items that should be included in a partnership agreement.
3. Explain what is meant by the term 'unlimited liability'.
4. Explain the difference between a limited partner and a general partner.
5. Describe what would happen in the absence of a partnership agreement.

 **DON'T FORGET**

Partnerships have unlimited liability.

 **DON'T FORGET**

A partnership can have 2–20 partners.

 **DON'T FORGET**

Partnerships are governed by the Partnership Act of 1890.

 **DON'T FORGET**

The partnership is dissolved if a partner leaves or dies.

DON'T FORGET

Decisions made by one partner are binding on all partners.

DON'T FORGET

Decision-making can be slowed down due to disagreements between partners.

DON'T FORGET

A limited partner contributes equity but is not responsible for any debts of the business.

 **ONLINE**

Find more exercises on partnership final accounts at www.brightredbooks.net

 ONLINE TEST

Test yourself on partnership final accounts at www.brightredbooks.net

EXERCISES ON PARTNERSHIP FINAL ACCOUNTS

EXERCISE 1

Black and White are in partnership sharing profits and losses in the ratio of 2:1 respectively. They both receive interest on equity of 10% and are charged 5% interest on drawings. Black also receives a salary of £15,000 per annum. White has also lent the business £12,000 for which she receives interest of 8%.

The following information is also available:

	Equity invested	Drawings for the year
Black	£40,000	£10,000
White	£20,000	£6,000

The profit for the year before taking any of the above into account amounted to £75,100.

Required:

1. Appropriation account of the partnership

2. Statement of Financial Position extract showing the 'financed by' section

3. Partners' equity and current accounts.

EXERCISE 2

Adams and Jones are in partnership sharing profits and losses in the ratio of 3:1 respectively. They both receive interest on equity of 10% and are charged 5% interest on drawings. Jones also receives a salary of £25,000 per annum. Adams has also lent the business £18,000 for which she receives interest of 6%.

The following information is also available:

	Equity invested	Drawings for the year
Adams	£50,000	£16,000
Jones	£30,000	£20,000

The profit for the year before taking any of the above into account amounted to £125,000.

Required:

1. Appropriation account of the partnership

2. Statement of Financial Position extract showing the 'financed by' section

3. Partners' equity and current accounts.

EXERCISE 3

Burns, Dickson and Murray are in partnership sharing profits and losses in the ratio of 3:2:1 respectively. The partners receive interest on equity of 10% and are charged 5% interest on drawings. Dickson also receives a salary

of £12,000 per annum. Murray has also lent the business £15,000 for which she receives interest of 7.5%.

The following information is also available:

	Equity invested	Drawings for the year
Burns	£60,000	£15,000
Dickson	£40,000	£20,000
Murray	£20,000	£10,000

The profit for the year before taking any of the above into account amounted to £165,000.

Required:

1. Appropriation account of the partnership

2. Statement of Financial Position extract showing the 'financed by' section

3. Partners' equity and current accounts.

EXERCISE 4

Findlay and Foye are in partnership sharing profits and losses equally.

The following is their trial balance as at 31 December Year 1.

	Dr	Cr
Premises	100,000	
Fixtures and fittings at cost	10,000	
Vehicles at cost	22,000	
Provision for depreciation: fittings		2,000
Provision for depreciation: vehicles		2,200
Trade receivables	18,240	
Trade payables		12,831
Cash and cash equivalents	3,895	
Sales revenue		128,550
Provision for bad debts		2,000
Discounts	1,250	1,000
VAT		4,500
Sales returns	550	
Electricity	800	
Rent and rates	1,250	
Wages and salaries	53,000	
Purchases	44,000	
Opening inventory	5,200	
Current accounts at 1 January Year 1		
Findlay		2,104
Foye		5,000
Equity accounts		
Findlay		60,000
Foye		40,000
Drawings		
Findlay	7,500	
Foye	12,500	
Loan from partner Foye		20,000
	£280,185	£280,185

Notes at 31 December Year 1

1. Closing inventory at 31 December Year 1 amounted to £6,300.

2. Electricity bill owing £200.

3. Rates paid in advance £250.

4. Wages owing £3,000.

contd

5. The provision for bad debts is to be maintained at 10% of trade receivables.

6. Depreciation is to be provided for as follows:

    (a) fixtures and fittings 10% on cost

    (b) vehicles 20% reducing balance.

7. Their partnership agreement states that:

    (a) interest on equity will be paid at 10% per annum

    (b) interest on drawings will be charged at 5% per annum

    (c) a partnership salary of £10,000 will be paid to Foye

    (d) interest on loans from partners will be paid at 5% per annum.

You are required to prepare, from the trial balance and notes:

1. Income Statement for the year ended 31 December Year 1 together with a Statement of Financial Position as at that date

2. the equity accounts of both partners

3. the current accounts of both partners.

EXERCISE 5

The following trial balance was extracted from the books of McManus and Keegan as at 31 December Year 2.

	Dr £	Cr £
Premises	90,000	
Fixtures and fittings at cost	5,600	
Vehicles at cost	32,000	
Provision for depreciation: fittings		1,250
Provision for depreciation: vehicles		7,500
Trade receivables	15,400	
Trade payables		9,627
Cash and cash equivalents		14,590
Sales revenue		114,560
Provision for bad debts		500
Discounts	750	1,200
VAT		5,600
Sales returns	260	
Bad debts	350	
Electricity	750	
Rent received		4,155
Rent and rates	940	
Wages and salaries	48,000	
Purchases	42,150	
Opening inventory	3,800	
Current accounts at 1 January Year 2		
McManus		6,483
Keegan		2,465
Equity accounts		
McManus		45,000
Keegan		25,000
Drawings		
McManus	8,000	
Keegan	10,000	
Loan from McManus		25,000
	£260,465	£260,465

Notes at 31 December Year 2

1. Closing inventory at 31 December Year 2 amounted to £8,250.

2. Rent receivable owing £200.

3. Rates paid in advance £240.

4. Wages owing £1,000.

5. The provision for bad debts is to be maintained at 5% of trade receivables.

6. Depreciation is to be provided for as follows:

    (a) fixtures and fittings 10% reducing balance

    (b) vehicles 15% on cost.

7. Their partnership agreement states that:

    (a) McManus and Keegan share profits and losses in the ratio of 3:2 respectively

    (b) interest on equity will be paid at 8% per annum

    (c) interest on drawings will be charged at 4% per annum

    (d) A partnership salary of £7,500 will be paid to Keegan

    (e) interest on loans from partners will be paid at 6% per annum.

You are required to prepare, from the trial balance and notes:

1. Income Statement for the year ended 31 December Year 2 together with a Statement of Financial Position as at that date

2. the equity accounts of both partners

3. the current accounts of both partners.

ONLINE

Find more exercises on partnership final accounts at www.brightredbooks.net

ONLINE TEST

Test yourself on partnership final accounts at www.brightredbooks.net

GOODWILL AND THE ADMISSION OF NEW PARTNERS

ONLINE

Head to www.brightredbooks.net for questions on this topic.

ONLINE TEST

Test yourself on goodwill and the admission of new partners at www.brightredbooks.net

DON'T FORGET

Goodwill is the amount paid for a business over and above the face value of its assets.

DON'T FORGET

When a new partner is admitted, the old partnership is dissolved.

DON'T FORGET

When a new partner is admitted, the assets of the business are revalued.

DON'T FORGET

Profits/losses on revaluation are shared among existing partners.

DON'T FORGET

Goodwill is written off between the new partners in their new profit-sharing ratio.

GOODWILL

A business is said to have a net worth of the total value of all its assets minus its liabilities at any given point. However, if the owner sells the business, they may be able to get a lot more for it than solely the face value of its assets. The main reason is that it is sold as a going concern and will continue to gain the new owner more of a return than if they bought all the assets separately.

Consider a business showing a net worth of £120,000 on its Statement of Financial Position which is subsequently sold for £150,000. The £30,000 that the new owner has paid over and above the value of the assets is known as **goodwill**.

Goodwill can arise for a variety of reasons. For example, if the business is in an excellent location; has a good customer base; has a strong brand; has guaranteed future sales; has a monopoly position; has ownership of patents or reputation.

Goodwill is shown as an intangible asset in the Statement of Financial Position. However, because it is difficult to place an exact value on, it is advisable to write it off. In a partnership, the question of goodwill arises when a partner leaves or dies or the business admits a new partner.

ADMISSION OF A NEW PARTNER

If a partnership decides to expand and needs investment, one option is to bring in a new partner. At that point, the business needs to be valued so that a fair amount can be agreed.

The revaluation of the business's assets will involve drawing up a Statement of Financial Position at that date, and a comparison will be made between the previous valuations of the various assets and the current valuation. Where the value has increased or decreased, existing partners will share the profit or loss on revaluation between them in their old profit-sharing ratio. This will all be completed before the new partner buys in.

Furthermore, it is also likely that the new partner will be charged a premium for goodwill, and this will go to the existing partners in their old profit-sharing ratio. At that point, it will be decided whether or not a **goodwill account** is to be kept – and, if not, the goodwill will be written off among the new partners in their new profit-sharing ratio.

Summary of procedures for introduction of a new partner

When a new partner is introduced, then the old partnership no longer exists and a new partnership agreement should be drawn up to reflect the details of the new partner, which will include a new profit-sharing ratio. It will be agreed that the new partner will receive a particular fraction or percentage of the profits, with the old partners sharing the remainder in their old profit-sharing ratios. In addition, the following will take place:

- a revaluation of the firm's assets takes place
- any profit or loss on revaluation is shared among existing partners
- if a premium is paid by the new partner for goodwill, it will be shared among existing partners in their old profit-sharing ratio
- if no goodwill account is to be kept, then it is written off between new partners in a new profit-sharing ratio
- the partners' equity accounts will be updated to reflect the above adjustments, which will also involve consolidating the existing partners' current accounts into their equity accounts.

contd

Example:

Martin and Jenkins are in partnership sharing profits and losses in the same ratio as their equity invested.

The equity and current account balances on 31 December Year 3 were as shown:

On 1 January Year 4, Martin and Jenkins agree to admit Bolton as a new partner under the following conditions.

1. Goodwill is to be valued at £15,000.
2. Bolton is to provide £30,000 as her equity.
3. A professional revaluation of the existing assets and liabilities results in this table:
4. Revaluation expenses amount to £2,000.
5. As a goodwill account is not to be kept, goodwill is to be written off against the equity accounts of the new partnership.
6. The balances on the original partners' current accounts are to be transferred to their equity accounts.
7. Bolton is to receive 10% of the profits, with the other partners continuing to share the remainder in the same relative proportions as before.

Martin and Jenkins have asked you to calculate on 1 January Year 4:

1. the profit or loss on revaluation;
2. the share of profit or loss on revaluation for each partner;
3. the new profit-sharing ratio;
4. the new equity balances of each partner.

	Equity account	Current account
	£	£
Martin	40,000	1,000 Cr
Jenkins	80,000	2,000 Dr

	Old value	New value
Fixtures	£20,000	£30,000
Vehicles	£45,000	£37,000
Debtors	£40,000	£50,000
Inventory	£8,000	£10,000

ONLINE

Find more exercises on goodwill and the admission of new partners at www.brightredbooks.net

Solution:

1. The profit or loss on revaluation:

Item	Effect on profit
Increase in value of fixtures	10,000
Decrease in value of vehicles	(8,000)
Increase in value of debtors	10,000
Increase in value of inventory	2,000
Revaluation expenses	(2,000)
Profit on revaluation	£12,000

This profit is shared between the two existing partners in their profit-sharing ratio in the ratio of equity invested, i.e.:
Martin : Jenkins
£40,000 : £80,000
= 4 : 8
= 1 : 2

2. Therefore the £12,000 is divided up as follows.
Martin 1/3 × £12,000 = £4,000
Jenkins 2/3 × £12,000 = £8,000
The payment for goodwill should also be shared between them in their profit-sharing ratio, i.e.:
Martin 1/3 × £15,000 = £5,000
Jenkins 2/3 × £15,000 = £10,000

3. The new profit-sharing ratio is calculated as follows.
Note 7 above stated that Bolton is to get 10% of the profits, with 'the other partners continuing to share the remainder in the same relative proportions as before'.
This is done as follows:
Bolton gets 10%
This leaves 90% to be shared by the others in their old profit-sharing ratio, therefore:
Martin gets 1/3 of 90% = 30%
Jenkins gets 2/3 of 90% = 60%
Therefore the new profit-sharing ratio is:
Martin 30%
Jenkins 60%
Bolton 10%

4. The new equity balances of each partner are calculated as follows.
Since no goodwill account is to be kept, the goodwill is now written off in the new profit-sharing ratio.
This has the effect of reducing the partners' equity accounts by that amount, because you are decreasing the value of the business.
In this example, the goodwill is £15,000, therefore we decrease

the partners' equity accounts as follows:
Martin 30% × 15,000 = £4,500
Jenkins 60% × 15,000 = £9,000
Bolton 10% × 15,000 = £1,500

	Martin	Jenkins	Bolton
Opening balances	40,000	80,000	30,000
Share of profit on revaluation	4,000	8,000	
Share of goodwill	5,000	10,000	
Current account balances	1,000	(2,000)	
TOTAL	50,000	96,000	30,000
Less goodwill written off	(4,500)	(9,000)	(1,500)
New equity balances	45,500	87,000	28,500

These can also be shown as ledger accounts as follows:

Equity account – Martin

	Dr	Cr	Bal	
Balance b/f		£40,000	£40,000	Cr
Revaluation		4,000	44,000	Cr
Goodwill		5,000	49,000	Cr
Current account		1,000	50,000	Cr
Goodwill	4,500		45,500	Cr

Equity account – Jenkins

	Dr	Cr	Bal	
Balance b/f		£80,000	£80,000	Cr
Revaluation		8,000	88,000	Cr
Goodwill		10,000	98,000	Cr
Current account	2,000		96,000	Cr
Goodwill	9,000		87,000	Cr

Equity account – Bolton

	Dr	Cr	Bal	
Bank		£30,000	£30,000	Cr
Goodwill	1,500		28,500	Cr

EXERCISES ON GOODWILL AND THE ADMISSION OF NEW PARTNERS

EXERCISE 1

Connell and Smith are in partnership and share profits and losses in the ratio of 3:2.

The equity and current account balances on 31 December were:

	Equity accounts £	Current accounts £
Connell	100,000	1,250
Smith	50,000	200 Dr

On 1 January, Connell and Smith agree to admit McGrath as a new partner under the following conditions.

1. Goodwill is to be valued at £20,000.
2. McGrath is to provide £30,000 as his equity.
3. A professional revaluation of the existing assets and liabilities takes place.

This results in:

	Old value £	New value £
Machinery	20,000	30,000
Fittings	25,000	24,000

4. Revaluation expenses are £1,000.
5. The balances on the original partners' current accounts are to be transferred to their equity accounts.
6. McGrath is to receive 25% of the profits, the other partners continuing to share the remainder in the same relative proportions as before.
7. As a goodwill account is not to be kept, goodwill is to be written off against the equity accounts of the new partnership.

Connell and Smith have asked you to calculate on 1 January:

1. the profit or loss on revaluation;
2. the share of profit or loss on revaluation for each partner;
3. the new profit-sharing ratio;
4. the new equity balances of each partner.

EXERCISE 2

Simpson and Stewart share profits and losses in the ratio of 5:3.

The equity and current account balances on 31 December were:

	Equity accounts £	Current accounts £
Simpson	£400,000	£2,500
Stewart	£150,000	£1,200 Dr

On 1 January, Simpson and Stewart agree to admit MacLellan as a new partner under the following conditions.

1. Goodwill is to be valued at £80,000.
2. MacLellan is to provide £100,000 as her equity.
3. A professional revaluation of the existing assets and liabilities takes place.

This results in:

	Old value £	New value £
Machinery	50,000	60,000
Fittings	40,000	30,000
Vehicles	20,000	18,000
Inventory	30,000	15,000
Premises	150,000	200,000

4. MacLellan is to receive 20% of the profits, the other partners continuing to share the remainder in the same relative proportions as before.
5. Revaluation expenses are £400.
6. As a goodwill account is not to be kept, goodwill is to be written off against the equity accounts of the new partnership.
7. The balances on the original partners' current accounts are to be transferred to their equity accounts.

Simpson and Stewart have asked you to calculate:

1. the profit or loss on revaluation;
2. the share of profit or loss on revaluation for each partner;
3. the new profit-sharing ratio;
4. the new equity balances of each partner.

EXERCISE 3

Downes and Law share profits and losses in the ratio of 2:1.

The equity and current account balances on 31 December were:

	Equity accounts	Current accounts
Downes	£50,000	£1,000
Law	£25,000	£300 Dr

On 1 January, Downes and Law agree to admit Woods as a new partner under the following conditions.

1. Goodwill is to be valued at £12,000.
2. Woods is to provide £15,000 as his equity.
3. A professional revaluation of the existing assets and liabilities takes place.

contd

This results in:

	Old value £	New value £
Premises	120,000	130,000
Inventory	18,000	17,000
Debtors	15,000	14,000
Vans	20,000	15,000

4. Revaluation expenses amounted to £300.
5. As a goodwill account is not to be kept, goodwill is to be written off against the equity accounts of the new partnership.
6. The balances on the original partners' current accounts are to be transferred to their equity accounts.
7. Woods is to receive 25% of the profits, the other partners continuing to share the remainder in the same relative proportions as before.

Downes and Law have asked you to calculate:

1. the profit or loss on revaluation;
2. the share of profit or loss on revaluation for each partner;
3. the new profit-sharing ratio;
4. the new equity balances of each partner.

EXERCISE 4

Nelson and McNab are in partnership sharing profits and losses in the ratio of equity invested. The following information is available at 1 January Year 2:

	Equity accounts	Current accounts
Nelson	£90,000	£1,500 Dr
McNab	£30,000	£1,000 Cr

Nelson has lent £10,000 to the partnership.

Their partnership agreement further states that:

1. interest on equity will be paid at 10% per annum;
2. interest on drawings is charged at 5%;
3. drawings for the year amounted to £7,000 for Nelson and £5,000 for McNab;
4. a partnership salary of £10,000 per annum is to be paid to Nelson;
5. all loans to the partnership will receive interest of 8% per annum.

The net profit for the year ended 31 December Year 2 was £72,000.

1. You are required to prepare for the year ended 31 December Year 2:
    (a) the appropriation account for the partnership;
    (b) the partners' current accounts.

On 1 January Year 3, Nelson and McNab decide to admit Williamson as a new partner under the following conditions.

1. Before Williamson is admitted as a partner, the assets are revalued resulting in a surplus of £5,400.
2. Williamson will contribute £40,000 to the partnership. This includes a premium of £8,000 for goodwill.

3. As a goodwill account is not to be kept, goodwill is to be written off against the equity accounts of the new partnership.
4. Williamson is to receive 1/5th share of profits, with Nelson and McNab continuing to share in the same ratio as before.

2. Calculate:
    (a) the new profit-sharing ratio;
    (b) the new opening equity account balances for each partner.

EXERCISE 5

Gallagher and Finnegan are in partnership sharing profits and losses in the ratio of equity invested. The following information is available at 1 January Year 2:

	Equity accounts	Current accounts
Gallagher	£100,000	£2,750 Cr
Finnegan	£25,000	£1,550 Dr

Finnegan has lent £15,000 to the partnership.

Their partnership agreement further states that:

1. interest on equity will be paid at 12% per annum;
2. interest on drawings is charged at 4%;
3. drawings for the year amounted to £6,500 for Gallagher and £8,000 for Finnegan;
4. a partnership salary of £12,000 per annum is to be paid to Gallagher;
5. all loans to the partnership will receive interest of 6% per annum.

The net profit for the year ended 31 December Year 3 was £67,000.

1. You are required to prepare for the year ended 31 December Year 2:
    (a) the appropriation account for the partnership;
    (b) the partners' current accounts.

On 1 January Year 3, Gallagher and Finnegan decide to admit Michael as a new partner under the following conditions.

1. Before Michael is admitted as a partner, the assets are revalued resulting in a loss on revaluation of £6,500.
2. Michael will contribute £30,000 to the partnership. This includes a premium of £10,000 for goodwill.
3. As a goodwill account is not to be kept, goodwill is to be written off against the equity accounts of the new partnership.
4. Michael is to receive a 25% share of profits, with Gallagher and Finnegan continuing to share in the same ratio as before.

2. Calculate:
    (a) the new profit-sharing ratio;
    (b) the new opening equity account balances for each partner.

MANUFACTURING ACCOUNTS

WHAT IS A MANUFACTURING ACCOUNT?

Manufacturing accounts are prepared by manufacturing businesses to show the cost of producing their goods.

A manufacturing account is prepared **before** the income statement. The cost of goods manufactured is transferred to the trading section of the income statement and replaces the figure for purchases which would be found if the business was buying and selling completed goods.

Examples of manufacturing concerns are white goods such as washing machines and fridges and everything from computers and cars to furniture and food.

Any business organisation which is involved in a manufacturing or production process should prepare a manufacturing account. The manufacturing account is used to show:

(a) the cost of the goods manufactured;

(b) the profit (or unusually the loss) on the manufacturing process.

Trading businesses purchase finished goods (from a wholesaler or cash and carry), but a manufacturing firm's purchases consist of raw materials that it uses in its manufacturing processes.

Examples of raw materials

TYPES OF COSTS SHOWN IN A MANUFACTURING ACCOUNT

A manufacturer needs to distinguish clearly between the different types of costs incurred in the production of its products – and the manufacturing account reflects this. Costs are divided into two types – **direct costs** and **indirect costs**.

Direct costs

These are the costs incurred which can be identified with the items being produced – they are part of the actual item being made. These costs include:

Direct materials	The raw materials actually used in the manufacture of the product, such as cloth used to produce shirts, flour used to produce bread, or wood used in the production of furniture.
Direct manufacturing wages	The wages of those workers actually engaged in the manufacturing process, such as the wages of a sewing-machine operator, baker or skilled craft worker.
Direct expenses	Expenses which can be traced directly to the units manufactured. Direct expenses can include royalties and licence fees etc. which have to be paid to other persons for the right to produce their products or to use their processes. They could also include the hire of specialised equipment to produce a unique batch of goods.

contd

DON'T FORGET

The manufacturing account is prepared **before** the income statement.

DON'T FORGET

A business involved in manufacturing the products it sells will purchase raw materials.

DON'T FORGET

Manufacturing costs are split into direct costs and indirect costs.

DON'T FORGET

Direct costs can be traced directly to the goods being manufactured.

DON'T FORGET

There are three main direct costs to consider when preparing a manufacturing account.

Prime cost

The prime cost is the total of all direct costs. Prime cost should be clearly labelled in the manufacturing account.

Prime cost = direct materials + direct manufacturing wages + direct expenses

Indirect costs

These are costs that are not directly related to the manufacturing process. However, without these costs it would be impossible to manufacture the products. These indirect costs are referred to as **overheads**. Examples include:

(a) factory light and heat   (c) factory manager's salary   (e) repairs

(b) store person's wages   (d) factory rent and rates   (f) general maintenance.

It is often the case that indirect costs, for example rent and rates or heat and light, have to be apportioned (shared) between the factory and other areas of the business, for example the office. The manufacturing account should only include the overheads that were incurred in the factory.

Work in progress (WIP)

When there is work in progress, that is, goods only part-completed at the beginning and end of an accounting period, an adjustment is needed.

Goods only part-complete at the end of an accounting period must be carried forward to the next accounting period, since this is when they will actually be completed.

Goods only part-complete at the beginning of the current accounting year must be dealt with in that period, since this is the accounting year in which they will become completed goods.

So, the general rule is:

- <u>Add</u> work in progress at the beginning of an accounting period.
- <u>Subtract</u> work in progress at the end of an accounting period.

DON'T FORGET

The total prime cost should be clearly labelled in the manufacturing account.

MANUFACTURING PROFIT

Manufacturing concerns like to compare their cost of manufacture with the wholesale cost of their output. They do this to see whether it has been more or less profitable to manufacture the product rather than purchase the items and sell them on.

The business will calculate the profit on manufacture by comparing the cost of manufacture with the wholesale cost of buying the same product.

ONLINE

Head to www.brightredbooks.net for questions and exercises on manufacturing accounts.

Example:

```
Profit on manufacture = wholesale cost of output – manufacturing cost of output
                      = £250,000 – £200,000
                      = £50,000
```

The profit on manufacture is added to the manufacturing cost of output in the manufacturing account, and the wholesale cost of the output is shown.

The wholesale cost-of-output figure is transferred to the income statement (increasing the cost of goods sold and so reducing gross profit), and the profit on manufacture is added to the gross profit figure (increasing the profit for the business).

ONLINE TEST

Test yourself on manufacturing accounts at www.brightredbooks.net

THINGS TO DO AND THINK ABOUT

1 Explain what is meant by prime cost.
2 Outline the procedures to be followed for dealing with work in progress when preparing a manufacturing account.
3 Explain what is meant by a manufacturing profit.

EXAMPLES OF MANUFACTURING ACCOUNTS

LAYOUT OF A MANUFACTURING ACCOUNT

Example:

McMillans Ltd
Manufacturing Account for the year ended 31 December Year 2

	£000s	£000s
Raw materials cost		
Opening inventory – raw materials		20
Add purchases – raw materials		240
		260
Add carriage – raw materials		5
		265
Less closing inventory – raw materials		15
COST OF RAW MATERIALS CONSUMED		250
Add direct costs		
Manufacturing wages		150
Direct expenses		10
PRIME COST OF MANUFACTURE		410
Add factory overheads		
Depreciation of factory machinery	5	
General expenses	42	
Factory rent and rates	25	
Indirect wages	10	82
		492
Add inventory – work in progress (WIP) at start		14
		506
Less inventory – work in progress (WIP) at end		20
FACTORY COST OF PRODUCTION		486
Add profit on manufacture		5
MARKET (WHOLESALE) VALUE OF FINISHED GOODS		491

TRANSFERS TO THE INCOME STATEMENT

Example:

McMillans Ltd
Income Statement for the Year ended 31 December Year 2

	£000s	£000s	£000s
Sales revenue			1,100
Less sales returns			50
Net sales revenue			1,050
Less cost of sales			
Opening inventory – finished goods		30	
Add market value (wholesale) value of finished goods		491	
		521	
Add purchases of finished goods		350	
		871	
Less closing inventory – finished goods		55	
COST OF SALES			816
Gross profit			234
Add profit on manufacture			5
			239

Note: In the unusual situation where a business made a **loss** on manufacture, the manufacturing loss would appear as an expense in the Income Statement.

DON'T FORGET

It is important to state the name of the business and the financial statement being prepared.

DON'T FORGET

Prime cost is the total of all direct costs.

DON'T FORGET

The manufacturing account should only include overheads that were incurred in the factory.

DON'T FORGET

Profit on manufacture is the difference between the factory cost of production and the wholesale value of finished goods.

DON'T FORGET

The wholesale value of finished goods is transferred from the manufacturing account to the Income Statement.

DON'T FORGET

The profit on manufacture is added to gross profit.

STATEMENT OF FINANCIAL POSITION

When preparing the Statement of Financial Position for a manufacturing concern, all inventories are shown in the 'current assets' section.

DON'T FORGET

All closing inventories are transferred to the 'current assets' section of the Statement of Financial Position.

Example:

McMillans Ltd
Statement of Financial Position as at 31 December Year 2

	£000s Cost	£000s Depreciation	£000s NBV
Non-current assets			
Property	326	−60	386
Equipment	25	2	23
Intangible assets:			
Goodwill			50
Preliminary expenses			10
			469
Current assets			
Closing inventory: Raw materials	15		
WIP	20		
Finished goods	20	55	
Trade receivables		39	
Electricity receivable		4	
		98	

THINGS TO DO AND THINK ABOUT

1. Prepare the manufacturing account of the Bannerman Trading Company for the year ended 31 December Year 2 from the following information.

	£
Inventory of raw materials at 1 January	500
Inventory of raw materials at 31 December	700
Raw materials purchased	8,000
Carriage inwards	200
Direct manufacturing wages	21,000
Royalties	150
Indirect wages	9,000
Rent of factory	440
Factory maintenance costs	400
General indirect expenses	310

ONLINE

For more exercises on manufacturing accounts, head to www.brightredbooks.net

2. Prepare a manufacturing account for the year ended 31 December Year 2 for the Brent Manufacturing Company from the following information.

	£
1 January inventory of raw materials	800
31 December inventory of raw materials	1,050
1 January inventory of work in progress	350
31 December inventory of work in progress	420
Direct wages	3,960
Indirect wages	2,550
Purchase of raw materials	8,700
Fuel and power	990
Direct expenses	140
Lubricants (oil for machinery)	300
Carriage inwards on raw materials	200
Rent of factory	720
Factory maintenance costs	420
Insurance of factory buildings	150
Transport expenses	180
General factory expenses	330

ONLINE TEST

Test yourself on manufacturing accounts at www.brightredbooks.net

EXERCISES ON MANUFACTURING ACCOUNTS

 EXERCISE 1

From the following list of balances, prepare a manufacturing account for the year ended 31 December Year 2 for TD Productions.

	£
Depreciation of factory machinery	620
Carriage inwards on raw materials	260
Raw materials purchased	10,100
Indirect wages	11,300
Direct manufacturing wages	22,000
Inventories:	
Raw materials 1 Jan	710
31 Dec	920
Work in progress 1 Jan	1,050
31 Dec	1,150
Factory rent	520
General factory expenses	400
Factory rates	420

800 finished units were produced. Calculate the manufacturing cost per unit.

EXERCISE 2

From the following information, prepare the manufacturing account for Unitsrus for the year ended 31 December Year 2.

	£
Raw materials purchased	7,000
Carriage inwards	200
Carriage outwards	250
Rent of office	50
Rent of factory	100
General office expenses	800
General factory expenses	600
Factory direct wages	5,000
Advertising	500
Travellers' salaries and commission	600
Bank charges	150
Office salaries	120
Sales	16,025
Factory indirect wages	400
Repairs and renewals to plant and machinery	275
Inventories:	
Raw materials 1 January	1,000
Raw materials 31 December	1,500
Finished goods 1 January	675
Finished goods 31 December	575
Work in progress 1 January	1,600
Work in progress 31 December	1,800

EXERCISE 3

From the information below, prepare a manufacturing account and an Income Statement (to gross profit) for Anytown Manufacturers for year ended 31 December Year 2.

	£
1 January inventory of raw materials	800
31 December inventory of raw materials	1,050
1 January inventory of work in progress	350
31 December stock of work in progress	420
Wages (direct)	3,960
Wages (indirect)	2,550
Purchase of raw materials	8,700
Fuel and power	990
Direct expenses	140
Lubricants	300
Carriage inwards on raw materials	200
Rent and rates of factory	720
Depreciation of factory plant and machinery	420
Internal transport expenses	180
Insurance of factory building and plant	150
General factory expenses	330

Additional information:

1. £3,500 inventory of finished goods at 1 Jan
2. £4,400 inventory of finished goods at 31 Dec
3. £25,000 sales of finished goods.

EXERCISE 4

From the following information, prepare the manufacturing account and the Income Statement of XYZ Co. as at 31 December Year 2.

	£
Inventory of raw materials at 1 Jan	2,100
Inventory of finished goods at 1 Jan	3,890
Work in progress at beginning	1,350
Direct wages	18,000
Indirect wages	14,500
Royalties	700
Carriage inwards on raw materials	350
Purchase of raw materials	37,000
Productive machinery (cost £28,000)	23,000
Accounting machinery (cost £2,000)	1,200
General factory expenses	3,100
Lighting and heating	750
Factory power	1,370
Administrative salaries	4,400
Sales force's salaries	3,000
Commission on sales	1,150
Rent and rates	1,200
Insurance	420

contd

General administrative expenses	1,340
Bank charges	230
Discounts allowed	480
Carriage outwards	490
Sales revenue	100,000
Trade receivables	14,230
Trade payables	12,500
Cash and cash equivalents	5,830
Drawings	2,000
Equity at 1 Jan	29,680

Additional information at 31 December:

1. Inventory of raw materials £2,400
    Inventory of finished goods £4,000
    Inventory of work in progress £1,500.
2. Lighting and heating and rent, rates and insurance to be apportioned:
    Factory 5/6; Administration 1/6.
3. Depreciation on productive and accounting machinery at 10% per annum on cost.

 **EXERCISE 5**

Gorleston Ltd is a manufacturing company, and the following details for the year ended 31 December Year 2

are extracted from its books.

	£
Inventory of raw materials at 1 Jan	23,265
Inventory of raw materials at 31 Dec	23,181
Inventory of manufactured goods at 1 Jan	45,284
Inventory of manufactured goods at 31 Dec	37,259
Work in progress at 1 Jan	14,285
Work in progress at 31 Dec	16,359
Purchase of raw materials	376,258
Manufacturing wages (direct)	188,950
Sales revenue	895,726
Factory expenses	24,825
Rent and rates of factory	13,000
Rent and rates of office	7,500
General administrative expenses	34,260
Sales force's salaries	18,590
Motor expenses	15,250
Other selling expenses	14,950
Depreciation of plant and machinery	10,000
Depreciation of motor vans	3,000

Prepare Gorleston's manufacturing account and Income Statement for the year ended 31 December Year 2.

 THINGS TO DO AND THINK ABOUT

Specimen exam-style exercise

McNair's manufactures gardening equipment. From the following information, prepare the manufacturing account and Income Statement for the year ended 31 December Year 2.

	£
Advertising	830
Bad debts	605
Bad-debt provision	1,000
Bank charges	120
Discount received	412
Discount allowed	100
Factory power	3,614
Fixtures and fittings	900
Factory expenses	205
Office expenses	346
Insurance	902
Light and heat	482
Plant and machinery 1 January	15,000
Plant and machinery added 30 June	2,000
Purchases of raw materials	33,668
Returns of raw materials	1,000
Carriage in	200
Rent and rates	1,486
Repairs to plant	785
Office salaries	3,690
Sales revenue	79,174
Inventories on 1 January:	
Raw materials	5,230
Finished goods	7,380
Work in progress	1,670
Direct factory wages	20,700
Carriage out	100

The following information has also to be accounted for:

1. Inventories at 31 December:
    Raw materials £3,560
    Work in progress £1,740
    Finished goods £9,650.
2. The following other payables have also to be accounted for:
    Factory power £562
    Rent and rates £386
    Light and heat £160
    General office expenses £40
    General factory expenses £25.
3. Other receivables: insurance £170.
4. Rent and rates, light and heat and insurance have to be allocated 5/6ths to the factory and 1/6th to the office.
5. You have also to provide for depreciation at 10% per annum for plant and machinery and 5% per annum for fixtures and fittings.
6. The bad-debt provision has to be increased by £500.

 ONLINE

For more exercises on manufacturing accounts, head to www.brightredbooks.net

 **ONLINE TEST**

Test yourself on manufacturing accounts at www.brightredbooks.net

INVESTMENT APPRAISAL 1

OVERVIEW

In order to improve the profitability of a company and to achieve capital growth, the company will need to invest in the business. This can mean such things as acquiring another company to expand their operations, or investing in new plant and machinery to modernise the factory and increase productivity and efficiency. These capital projects often run into millions of pounds and need to be carefully considered before the decision to invest is made.

Sometimes the company has to decide between two or more projects. In order to choose one, they all need to be analysed.

Various techniques exist to measure the potential success of projects regarding how long they will take to pay for themselves and start to turn a profit.

THE ACCOUNTING RATE OF RETURN METHOD

The **accounting rate of return** from a project is the average earnings from a project (after tax and depreciation) divided by the original cost of the project **or** the cost of the project averaged over its life.

DON'T FORGET

Depreciation = Cost – Residual scrap value ÷ number of years of life of the project.

DON'T FORGET

Using the ARR method, we are interested in the profits flowing from the investment.

DON'T FORGET

The preferred method of calculating ARR = average earnings from a project (after tax and depreciation) divided by the original cost of the project.

Example:

Ramsay Rodgers plc is considering investing in new machinery costing £50,000. The machinery will have a projected life of 5 years and be scrapped at the end of that period, when it will have no sales value. Tax should be deducted on profits at a rate of 25%. The projected cash inflows from the project are as follows:

Year	Cash inflow £
1	30,000
2	45,000
3	45,000
4	35,000
5	15,000
	£170,000

The total cash inflow from this project is £170,000. However, we are interested in the profit flowing from the project, and this can be worked out by first determining the net inflows from the project, then working out the depreciation and tax and deducting them from the inflows.

Depreciation = Cost – Residual scrap value ÷ number of years of life of the project
In this case:
£50,000 – 0 ÷ 5 = £10,000 per year.
Second, we need to use this information to determine the average income from the investment. This is shown in the following table:

Year	Cash inflow	Depreciation	Profit before tax	Profit after tax of 25%
1	£30,000	£10,000	£20,000	£15,000
2	£45,000	£10,000	£35,000	£26,250
3	£45,000	£10,000	£35,000	£26,250
4	£35,000	£10,000	£25,000	£18,750
5	£15,000	£10,000	£5,000	£3,750
Total profit after depreciation and tax				**£90,000**

Third, we need to calculate the ARR by dividing the average profit by **either** the original investment **or** the average investment.
Method 1 – Dividing by the original investment (preferred)
Average profit = 90,000/5 = £18,000
ARR = 18,000/50,000 × 100 = 36%.
Method 2 – Dividing by the average investment
Average capital expenditure = £50,000/5 = £10,000
ARR = 18,000/10,000 = 180%.
These figures should now be used to compare between projects, where the project with the higher ARR would be the chosen course of action.

contd

Using ARR to compare two or more projects with different time periods

Example:

Mill Hill plc is considering investing in either Project A or Project B, where these have different time periods: Project A is 6 years, and Project B is 3 years. The table contains information relating to both projects:

		Project A	Project B
		£	£
Capital outlay		120,000	120,000
Net cash inflows	Year 1	50,000	50,000
After tax and	Year 2	40,000	40,000
depreciation	Year 3	30,000	60,000
	Year 4	30,000	–
	Year 5	13,000	–
	Year 6	5,000	–

Average profits from Project A = 168,000/6 = £28,000
Average profits from Project B = 150,000/3 = £50,000

Using Method 1 – dividing by the original investment

ARR = Average profits/original investment × 100

Project A	Project B
ARR = 28,000/120,000 × 100	ARR = 50,000/120,000 × 100
= 23.33%	= 33.33%

Using Method 2 – dividing by the average investment

Average investment for both projects = 120,000/6 = 20,000
ARR = Average profits/average investment × 100

Project A	Project B
ARR = 28,000/20,000 × 100	ARR = 50,000/20,000 × 100
= 140%	= 250%

Both methods show Project B to have the higher rate of return – and this would then be the chosen course of action for the company.

While this method of investment appraisal is commonly used in the real world and has its advantages, it is very simplistic and is not preferred by the accounting profession because of its limitations.

Advantages of ARR

- it is an identifiable and familiar profitability ratio similar to Return on Capital Employed, which makes it easy for managers with limited financial training to understand
- it is easy to calculate
- it emphasises the need to make a profit.

Disadvantages of ARR

- it does not take into consideration the time value of money
- it ignores the timing of cash outflows and inflows
- there is no target rate of return
- it is unreliable if timescales are different
- it may lead to choosing a project which gains high profits in earlier years and passing up on a project that will only begin to maximise profits in later years.

 **DON'T FORGET**

ARR is unreliable for projects which have varying timescales.

 ONLINE

Practise your accounting skills by completing the further exercises at www.brightredbooks.net

 ONLINE TEST

Head to www.brightredbooks.net to test yourself on investment appraisal.

 THINGS TO DO AND THINK ABOUT

1. Explain why it is necessary for firms to use investment appraisal.
2. State the two methods for calculating the accounting rate of return.
3. Outline one advantage of the ARR method of investment appraisal.
4. Outline one disadvantage of the ARR method of investment appraisal.
5. Describe in your own words how the ARR method of investment appraisal is calculated.

INVESTMENT APPRAISAL 2

THE PAYBACK METHOD

The **payback period** is the term commonly given to the amount of time a project takes to pay for itself.

This is another popular method, mainly due to its simplicity. In this method, cash inflows are accumulated until they equal the amount of the initial investment, after which they are ignored. The best project using this method is the one which pays for itself the quickest, therefore the tendency is for managers to be drawn to projects with high returns in the early years.

DON'T FORGET

The best project is the one which pays for itself quickest.

Example 1:

High Rollers plc is considering a project which has an initial cost of £25,000. The following table contains the estimated cash flows over a 5-year period.

	Cash inflows £	Running total £
Year 1	12,000	12,000
Year 2	8,000	20,000
Year 3	5,000	25,000
Year 4	4,000	Ignore
Year 5	4,000	Ignore

The total cash inflows will equal £25,000 after year 3, and the cash inflows in years 4 and 5 are ignored. The payback period is therefore 3 years.

Example 2:

Melville plc is considering investing in one of two mutually exclusive projects. The initial outlay for each project is £60,000.

		Project A £	Project B £
Cash outlay		60,000	60,000
Cash inflow	Year 1	20,000	28,000
	Year 2	16,000	22,000
	Year 3	16,000	10,000
	Year 4	8,000	8,000
	Year 5	4,000	–

DON'T FORGET

Cash inflows after payback are ignored.

The payback period is calculated as follows:

	Project A £		Project B £	
Cash outlay	**60,000**		**60,000**	

Cash inflows	Annual £	Cumulative £	Annual £	Cumulative £
Year 1	20,000	**20,000**	28,000	**28,000**
Year 2	16,000	**36,000**	22,000	**50,000**
Year 3	16,000	**52,000**	10,000	**60,000**
Year 4	8,000	**60,000**	8,000	**68,000**
Year 5	4,000	**64,000**		

DON'T FORGET

This method can lead managers to favour investments which have high returns in the short term, passing up on a project that will only begin to maximise profits in later years.

Time taken to pay back capital

	4 years	**3 years**

In the above case, Project B has the shorter payback period and therefore will be the one that is chosen. However, on examining the table, the disadvantages of ignoring cashflows after payback are obvious.

Again, this method of investment appraisal is commonly used in the real world and has a few advantages. However, it is also very simplistic and has some disadvantages in common with ARR.

contd

Calculating the payback method to the nearest day

Sometime it is necessary to calculate the payback period to the nearest day, particularly when competing projects pay for themselves in the same year. This is due to the fact that the payback date may fall during a financial year and not conveniently at the end of the year. For example, consider the following project.

Example:

		Cash inflow £	Cumulative £
Cash outlay		55,000	
Cash inflow	Year 1	20,000	20,000
	Year 2	16,000	36,000
	Year 3	16,000	52,000
	Year 4	8,000	60,000
	Year 5	4,000	ignore

In this case, the payback period is reached some time during year 4. In order to ascertain how many days into year 4 this works out at, we have to calculate:
- The cash inflow for year 4 = £8,000
- How much money we need in year 4 to achieve payback = £3,000
- The money we need as a proportion of the inflow for year 4 = £3,000 ÷ £8,000.

Then all we have to do is apply this fraction to the number of days in the year, as follows:
$3/8 \times 365 = 136.875 = 137$ days (to the nearest day)
Therefore the payback period in this case = 3 years 137 days

Advantages of payback

- Very easy to understand and calculate
- Easy comparison can be made between mutually exclusive projects
- May encourage growth by favouring projects providing a quick return
- Reduces the time during which liquidity is at risk
- Considers cash flows rather than profit.

Disadvantages of payback

- Calculation and timing of net cash flows may be difficult
- Ignores profitability
- Ignores net cash inflows after payback period
- Ignores the time value of money.

ONLINE

Practise your accounting skills by completing the further exercises at www.brightredbooks.net

ONLINE TEST

Head to www.brightredbooks.net to test yourself on investment appraisal.

 THINGS TO DO AND THINK ABOUT

1. Explain why managers using the payback method of investment appraisal may be drawn to short-term investments.

2. Outline the main limitations of using the payback method of investment appraisal.

3. Explain why is it sometimes necessary to calculate the payback period to the nearest day.

4. Describe one advantage of using the payback method of investment appraisal.

5. Describe in your own words how the payback method of investment appraisal is calculated.

EXERCISES ON INVESTMENT APPRAISAL

 EXERCISE 1

Richardson plc is considering investing in new machinery costing £40,000. The machinery will have a projected life of 5 years and will be scrapped at the end of that period, when it will have no sales value. Tax should be deducted on profits at a rate of 25%. The projected cash inflows from the project are as follows:

Year	Cash inflow £
1	15,000
2	22,500
3	22,500
4	17,500
5	10,500
	£88,000

Calculate the Accounting Rate of Return using both methods, i.e.

1. dividing by the **original** investment
2. dividing by the **average** investment.

 EXERCISE 2

Anderson Manufacturing plc is considering investing in new machinery costing £60,000. The machinery will have a projected life of 5 years and will be scrapped at the end of that period, when it will have no sales value. Tax should be deducted on profits at a rate of 25%. The projected cash inflows from the project are as follows:

Year	Cash inflow £
1	20,000
2	35,000
3	35,000
4	25,000
5	5,000
	£120,000

Calculate the Accounting Rate of Return using both methods, i.e.

1. dividing by the **original** investment
2. dividing by the **average** investment.

 EXERCISE 3

Robinson plc is considering investing in new machinery costing £60,000. The projected cash inflows from the project are as follows:

Year	Cash inflow £
1	15,000
2	22,500
3	22,500
4	17,500
5	10,500
	£88,000

Calculate the payback period for the project.

 EXERCISE 4

Williams plc is considering investing in new machinery costing £75,000. The projected cash inflows from the project are as follows:

Year	Cash inflow £
1	20,000
2	35,000
3	35,000
4	25,000
5	5,000
	£120,000

Calculate the payback period for the project to the nearest day.

 EXERCISE 5

Halston plc is considering investing in either Project A or Project B, where both projects are mutually exclusive.

The following data relates to the 2 projects.

	Project A £	Project B £
Initial cost	150,000	150,000
Cash inflows		
Year 1	75,000	40,000
Year 2	60,000	55,000
Year 3	45,000	60,000
Year 4	40,000	65,000
Year 5	25,000	65,000

Advise the company which project they should invest in, using the payback method to the nearest day.

 EXERCISE 6

Parkview plc is considering investing in some new machinery. The machinery will have a projected life of 5 years and will be scrapped at the end of that period, when it will have no sales value. Tax should be deducted on profits at a rate of 25%. The projected cash inflows from the alternative options are as follows:

	Machine 1 £	Machine 2 £
Initial cost	120,000	120,000
Cash inflows		
Year 1	55,000	40,000
Year 2	40,000	30,000
Year 3	35,000	35,000
Year 4	20,000	35,000
Year 5	5,000	10,000

1. Advise the company of which machine to invest in, using the Accounting Rate of Return (based on average profits earned on the initial investment).
2. Calculate the payback period to the nearest day for each machine.

contd

 **EXERCISE 7**

Nilsson plc is considering investing in some new machinery. The machinery will have a projected life of 5 years and will be scrapped at the end of that period, when it will have no sales value. Tax should be deducted on profits at a rate of 25%. The projected cash inflows from the alternative options are as follows:

	Machine 1 £	Machine 2 £
Initial cost	240,000	240,000
Cash inflows		
Year 1	100,000	90,000
Year 2	80,000	70,000
Year 3	70,000	55,000
Year 4	40,000	45,000
Year 5	25,000	40,000

1. Calculate the Accounting Rate of Return (based on average profits earned on the initial investment).
2. Calculate the Accounting Rate of Return (based on average profits earned on the average investment).
3. Calculate the payback period to the nearest day for each machine.

 EXERCISE 8

Davies plc is considering investing in some new equipment. The equipment will have a projected life of 5 years and will be scrapped at the end of that period, when it will have no sales value. Tax should be deducted on profits at a rate of 25%. The projected cash inflows from the alternative options are as follows:

	Equipment 1 £	Equipment 2 £
Initial cost	300,000	300,000
Cash inflows		
Year 1	120,000	100,000
Year 2	85,000	100,000
Year 3	75,000	95,000
Year 4	60,000	65,000
Year 5	45,000	55,000

1. Calculate the Accounting Rate of Return (based on average profits earned on the initial investment).
2. Calculate the Accounting Rate of Return (based on average profits earned on the average investment).
3. Calculate the payback period to the nearest day for each project.

 EXERCISE 9

Salamander plc is considering investing in some new machinery. The machinery will have a projected life of 5 years and will be scrapped at the end of that period, when it will have no sales value. Tax should be deducted on profits at a rate of 25%. The projected cash inflows from the alternative options are as follows:

	Machine 1 £	Machine 2 £
Initial cost	150,000	150,000
Cash inflows		
Year 1	70,000	40,000
Year 2	60,000	60,000
Year 3	50,000	70,000
Year 4	40,000	40,000
Year 5	30,000	30,000

1. Advise the company of which machine to invest in using the Accounting Rate of Return (based on average profits earned on the initial investment).
2. Calculate the Accounting Rate of Return (based on average profits earned on the average investment).
3. Calculate the payback period to the nearest day for each machine.

THINGS TO DO AND THINK ABOUT

1. Describe how a large company might use investment appraisal in decision-making.
2. Outline one similarity and one difference between the Accounting Rate of Return and the payback method of investment appraisal.
3. Explain the difference between cash flow and profitability.
4. Describe the method of investment appraisal which focuses on profitability rather than cash inflows.
5. Explain what is meant by the phrase 'ignores the time value of money'.

ONLINE

Find the answers to these exercises and one further exercise at www.brightredbooks.net

ONLINE TEST

Head to www.brightredbooks.net to test yourself on investment appraisal.

INVESTMENT RATIOS 1

AN OVERVIEW

It is usual practice for a business enterprise – such as a public limited company – to produce a set of final accounts at the end of a specific period to gauge financial performance within the business. A range of stakeholders will be interested in these accounts, for example managers, employees, owners, lenders, the government, shareholders and customers.

The final accounts that are produced – normally the Income Statement and Statement of Financial Position – only give a historical record for that financial period. Greater analysis of these results is required to judge if the business has improved on last year's performance or performed in line with budgeted forecasts or in line with competitors.

To enhance the information gathered from the final accounts, a business will carry out some form of ratio analysis.

Results will be compared in three separate areas:

- profitability
- liquidity
- efficiency.

As well as using profitability, liquidity and efficiency ratios, investors or potential investors within a business will also be interested in a range of additional ratios called **investment ratios**. These can analyse the financial performance of a business further.

Investment ratios provide additional financial information for any stakeholder who has a general interest in investing or who has invested in a public limited company.

The five main investment ratios and the formula used to calculate them are shown in the table below.

Name of ratio	Formula
Equity gearing ratio	(Preference shares + Debentures (or long-term loans)) : Ordinary shares
Dividend yield	$\frac{\text{Ordinary dividend per share}}{\text{Market price per share}} \times 100$
Dividend cover	$\frac{\text{(Net profit – Preference dividends)}}{\text{Dividend on ordinary shares}}$
Earnings per share	$\frac{\text{(Net profit – Preference dividends)}}{\text{Number of ordinary shares}}$
Price/earnings ratio	$\frac{\text{Market price per share}}{\text{Earnings per share}}$

EQUITY GEARING RATIO

(Preference shares + Long term loans) : Ordinary shares

This is the relationship between the ordinary share equity of a company and the equity which gives a **fixed** return – **preference shares** and **debentures**.

A **highly geared** company is one which has a **high** proportion of fixed-interest equity in relation to ordinary share equity or vice versa. A highly geared company suggests a greater exposure because there are interest charges to be paid and loan repayments due, the payment of which is not optional. In times of **HIGH** profits, funds borrowed at relatively low or fixed interest rates will enhance available profits and make the payment of relatively higher ordinary dividends possible. When profits are **LOW**, funds borrowed at relatively high or fixed interest rates will reduce profits available for distribution and make high ordinary dividends unlikely.

contd

Where a company has a large number of preference shares and debentures, it is committed to paying the dividends and interest to those investors first, and so the possibility of paying high dividends to ordinary shareholders is less likely. On the other hand, a company whose equity is made up almost entirely of ordinary shares has little or no commitment to pay preference dividends or interest, and the probability of high dividends for ordinary shareholders becomes more possible.

If a **low-geared** company earns high rates of return, then the ordinary shareholder will gain, but if profits are low they may receive no dividend. Therefore, a low-geared company would be more likely to attract the 'get-rich-quick' type of investor who is prepared to risk his/her investment.

Low gearing has the advantage that directors have greater flexibility in appropriating profits, and there is less risk for ordinary shareholders as there is no priority to pay preference share dividends or debenture interest.

A company with only ordinary share equity is **ungeared**. The following principles usually apply:

- A business with a gearing ratio of **more than 50%** is traditionally said to be 'highly geared'.
- A business with gearing of **less than 25%** is traditionally described as having 'low gearing'.
- Something between 25% and 50% would be considered normal for a well-established business which is happy to finance its activities using a degree of debt.

It is important to remember that financing a business through long-term debt is not necessarily a bad thing! Long-term debt is normally cheap, and it reduces the amount that shareholders have to invest in the business.

How do you reduce gearing?

Shareholders and management can decide to reduce gearing by:

- repaying long term loans;
- retaining profits rather than issuing dividends;
- issuing more shares;
- converting debentures or other loans into shares.

How do you increase gearing?

Shareholders and management could increase gearing through:

- buying back ordinary shares;
- issuing preference shares or debentures;
- converting short-term debt into longer-term loans.

 THINGS TO DO AND THINK ABOUT

Problem-solving: gearing ratio

Grants plc has the following equity structure:

5% debentures (2025) of £80,000

3% preference shares of £1 each, £100,000

Ordinary shares of £1 each, £80,000

During financial Year 4, profit for the year was much higher than expected. Explain why this may be good news for ordinary shareholders.

If profit for the year falls considerably during Year 5, explain why ordinary shareholders may be very concerned about returns on their shares.

INVESTMENT RATIOS 2

DIVIDEND YIELD

$$\frac{\text{Ordinary dividend per share}}{\text{Market price per share}} \times 100$$

DON'T FORGET

Dividend yield measures the real rate of return on an investment by comparing dividend paid to the market price of the share.

This measures the **real** rate of return on an investment in shares, as distinct from the declared dividend rate (which is based on the nominal value of the share), by comparing the dividend paid against the market price of the share. Dividend yield allows investors to compare the return on their investment with that of bank accounts. Investors would have to decide whether any additional return is worth the risk of investing in shares in the business.

A decrease in dividend yield could be a result of:

- a reduction in proposed ordinary dividend per share
- the market price of the ordinary share increasing
- a decision made by directors to transfer profits back into the business in the form of unappropriated profits.

DIVIDEND COVER

$$\frac{(\text{Net profit} - \text{Preference dividends})}{\text{Dividends on ordinary shares}}$$

DON'T FORGET

Dividend cover shows how many times the profit for the year after tax covers the dividend paid.

This compares the **amount of profit earned per ordinary share** with the **amount of dividend paid**, thereby showing the proportion of profits that were distributed to ordinary shareholders and the proportion of profits that were retained in the business for future expansion.

In simple terms, dividend cover is the number of times the profit out of which dividends may be paid covers the dividend.

The higher the answer, the less likely it is that future dividends will be cut due to a fall in profits. On the other hand, if the cover is too high, shareholders may decide that the directors are adopting a mean dividend policy.

A decrease in dividend yield could be a result of:

- dividend on ordinary shares being paid to a larger number of shareholders
- a fall in profit for the year after tax.

EARNINGS PER SHARE

$$\frac{(\text{Net profit} - \text{Preference dividends})}{\text{Number of ordinary shares}}$$

This is the most frequently used of all the accounting ratios and is generally felt to give a better view of performance to potential investors than either the dividend cover or the dividend yield. It expresses profit in terms of ordinary shares issued.

It indicates how much of a company's profit can be attributed to each ordinary share in the company.

It enables comparison between year-to-year earnings.

A decrease in dividend yield could be a result of:

- net profit for the year after tax falling
- an increase in the number of ordinary shares.

PRICE/EARNINGS RATIO

$$\frac{\text{Market price per share}}{\text{Earnings per share}}$$

This relates the **earnings per share** to the **market price of the share**. It simply calculates the number of times the price being paid for the share on the stock market exceeds the earnings of the share.

It is a useful indicator of how the stock market assesses the company. The market price of the share is determined by the **demand** for it on the stock market in relation to its **supply**.

It also depends as much on future prospects as on past results, therefore what the shareholder is really buying is a share of future profits.

It is also very useful when a company proposes an issue of new shares, in that it enables potential investors to better assess whether the expected future earnings make the share a worthwhile investment.

The greater the price/earnings ratio, the greater the demand for the shares.

A decrease in price/earnings ratio could be a result of increases in earnings per share.

DON'T FORGET

This ratio compares earning per share to the price paid for the share on the stock market.

THINGS TO DO AND THINK ABOUT

1. Explain what is meant by the term 'final accounts'.
2. Identify the stakeholders who would be interested in the final accounts of a public limited company.
3. Explain the difference between a highly geared company and a low-geared company.
4. Outline strategies that could be adopted by a public limited company to reduce its gearing ratio.
5. Describe the information that would be gained from calculating the following ratios:
   (a) earnings per share.
   (b) price/earnings ratio.

ONLINE

For some activities on investment ratios, head to www.brightredbooks.net

ONLINE TEST

Test yourself on investment ratios at www.brightredbooks.net

EXERCISES ON INVESTMENT RATIOS

EXERCISE 1

Three companies – Earth plc, Wind plc and Fire plc – have the same total equity but made up from the sources indicated below.

	Earth plc	Wind plc	Fire plc
	£	£	£
8% debentures	500,000	Nil	Nil
7% preference shares	700,000	800,000	300,000
Ordinary shares of £1	600,000	1,000,000	1,500,000
	£1,800,000	£1,800,000	£1,800,000
Ordinary share market value	£1.20	£1.50	£2.00
Ordinary share dividend declared	20p	15p	10p

1. (a) Calculate the gearing ratio for each of the three companies.
   (b) State which company has the lowest gearing, and explain why.
   (c) Which company would be most attractive to the ordinary shareholder when business conditions are good? Give a reason for your answer.

2. (a) For each company, calculate the profits available for ordinary shareholders if each of the companies made a profit of £360,000 before charging interest on debentures and tax of £60,000.
   (b) For each company, calculate the earnings per ordinary share (answer to the nearest penny).
   (c) Calculate the price/earnings ratio for each company (answer to one decimal place).

3. For each company, calculate the:
   (a) dividend yield
   (b) dividend cover.

EXERCISE 2

The following table gives information about the financing of three companies.

	Rock plc	Paper plc	Scissors plc
	£	£	£
10% debentures	300,000	Nil	Nil
5% preference shares	50,000	200,000	150,000
Ordinary shares of £1	250,000	400,000	450,000
	£600,000	£600,000	£600,000
Ordinary share market value	£2.50	£2.00	£1.25
Ordinary share dividend declared	25p	20p	15p

1. (a) Calculate the gearing ratio for each of the three companies.
   (b) State which company has the lowest gearing, and explain why.

(c) Which company would be most attractive to the ordinary shareholder when business conditions are good? Give a reason for your answer.

3. (a) For each company, calculate the profits available for ordinary shareholders, if each of the companies made a profit of £330,000 before charging interest on debentures and tax of £90,000.
   (b) For each company, calculate the earnings per ordinary share (answer to the nearest penny).
   (c) Calculate the price/earnings ratio for all three companies (answer to one decimal place).

4. Calculate, for each of the three companies, the:
   (a) dividend yield
   (b) dividend cover (answer to one decimal place).

EXERCISE 3

Three companies – Lock plc, Stock plc and Barrel plc – have the same total equity but are financed differently as shown below.

	Lock plc	Stock plc	Barrel plc
	£	£	£
5% debentures	200,000	Nil	Nil
5% preference shares	400,000	450,000	300,000
Ordinary shares of £1	400,000	550,000	700,000
	£1,000,000	£1,000,000	£1,000,000
Ordinary share market value	£1.50	£2.50	£3.00
Ordinary share dividend declared	15p	24p	20p

For each of the three companies, you are required to:

1. (a) calculate the gearing ratio;
   (b) identify which company has the lowest gearing and explain why;
   (c) say what factors an ordinary shareholder, interested in receiving a good return on her/his investment, will consider when deciding which company to invest in.

For each of the three companies, you are required to calculate:

2. (a) the profits available for ordinary shareholders, if each of the companies made a profit of £650,000 before charging interest on debentures and tax of £175,000;
   (b) the earnings per ordinary share (answer to the nearest penny);
   (c) the price/earnings ratio (answer to one decimal place);

3. (a) dividend yield (answer to one decimal place);
   (b) dividend cover (answer to one decimal place).

contd

WHY IS RATIO ANALYSIS OF INTEREST?

- Ratio analysis enables users of financial statements to draw conclusions concerning the financial wellbeing and performance of the reporting entity.
- Ratio analysis can be used to review trends and compare business entities with each other.
- Independent auditors can review the manner in which the data has been presented and provide a filter mechanism attesting to the reliability of the information presented.
- Without ratios, financial statements would be largely uninformative to all but the very skilled. With ratios, financial statements can be interpreted and usefully applied to satisfy the needs of the reader.

- There are many parties interested in analysing financial statements; shareholders, lenders, customers, suppliers, employees, government agencies and competitors are just a few, although they will all be interested in different things.
- Ratio analysis is the first step in assessing an entity. It removes some of the mystery surrounding financial statements and makes it easier to pinpoint items which it would be interesting to investigate further.
- Investors are unlikely to invest in a business unless they can analyse information to determine the risk associated with any potential investment.

THINGS TO DO AND THINK ABOUT

Specimen exam-style question

The following are the final accounts of Donnelly & Wilson Plc for Year 1 and Year 2.

INCOME STATEMENTS FOR YEAR ENDING 31 DECEMBER

	YEAR 1 £	YEAR 1 £	YEAR 2 £	YEAR 2 £
Gross profit		480,000		744,000
Expenses		120,000		130,000
		360,000		614,000
Add other income				
Interest on debentures		15,000		5,000
Profit for the year before taxation		345,000		609,000
Corporation yax		86,250		152,250
Profit for the year after taxation		258,750		456,750
Add unappropriated profit		4,000		6,250
		262,750		463,000
Ordinary dividend	13,500		36,000	
Preference dividend	3,000		3,000	
		16,500		39,000
Unappropriated profit		£246,250		£424,000

STATEMENTS OF FINANCIAL POSITION AS AT 31 DECEMBER

	YEAR 1 £	YEAR 1 £	YEAR 2 £	YEAR 2 £
Non-current assets		1,554,000		2,000,000
Current assets				
Inventory	220,000		250,000	
Trade receivables	120,000		160,000	
Cash and cash equivalents	20,000		25,250	
	360,000		435,250	
Less current liabilities				
Trade payables	65,500		101,000	
Corporation tax	86,250		152,250	
Debenture interest due	15,000		5,000	
Wages payable			3,000	
	167,750	192,250	261,250	174,000
		1,746,250		2,174,000
Non-current liabilities				
5% debentures		300,000		100,000
		£1,446,250		£2,074,000
Equity				
Ordinary shares of £1 each	150,000		300,000	
6% preference shares of £1 each	50,000	200,000	50,000	350,000
Reserves				
Share premium			60,000	
Profit and loss account	1,246,250	1,246,250	1,664,000	1,724,000
		£1,446,250		£2,074,000

Note: The market value of the ordinary shares was £2.10 in Year 1 and £3 in Year 2.

You are required to calculate the following ratios for each year (correct to 2 decimal places) and suggest possible reasons for any differences.

1. Dividend yield;
2. Dividend cover;
3. Earnings per share;
4. Price/earnings ratio;
5. Equity gearing ratio.

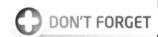

DON'T FORGET

You should attempt some of these exercises by means of a spreadsheet using appropriate formulae.

ONLINE

For extra activities on investment ratios, head to www.brightredbooks.net

ONLINE TEST

Test yourself on investment ratios at www.brightredbooks.net

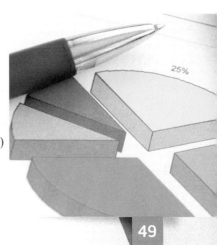

PREPARING MANAGEMENT ACCOUNTING INFORMATION

THE MANAGEMENT ACCOUNTANT

While financial accounting is concerned with recording and reporting financial information to stakeholders outwith the organisation, management accounting is focused on collecting high-quality information within the business so that the company can improve and operate more efficiently and effectively.

As a result, the management accountant will be concerned with collecting and analysing costs and revenues of current and future activities in order to aid decision-making.

ROLE OF THE MANAGEMENT ACCOUNTANT

The main activities of the management accountant are as follows:

- design, implement and manage information systems in order to produce reports which will help the organisation to monitor and manage its performance and to plan future activities
- work as part of a management team involving managers from other areas of the business such as marketing and human resources and production
- supply financial information to other departments to assist them in their own internal planning and decision-making
- provide advice to assist management with decision-making regarding alternative strategies and courses of action
- producing business plans, forecasts and budgeting information.

Advantages of management accounting

The main advantages of management accounting are as follows:

- The most and least profitable products can be identified
- The most and least profitable departments or areas of the business can be identified
- Areas where costs are too high can be identified and action taken
- The business will have more control over costs
- The business can plan production in a way that maximises profits.

This means that the information gathered will help management to make clearer decisions such as whether to lay off workers, or change suppliers of materials or services; whether to make or buy products or even close a department.

THE COST ACCOUNTANT

In order to make these good decisions, it is essential that the exact costs of products, services and activities of the business are known. This activity is known as **cost accounting**. In order to do this, the cost accountant will adopt various techniques such as job costing, unit costing, service costing, contribution analysis and process costing. The results of these techniques are then passed on to management in order that decisions can be made.

The main duties of the cost accountant are as follows:

- collecting and categorising costs such as labour, material and expenses
- allocating costs to cost centres
- costing of products and services
- determining the profit made on individual products
- drawing up budgets and making comparisons between budgeted and actual data.

Cost centres

A cost centre is any area of a business to which costs can be allocated. It can be a department, person, product or activity, e.g. sales department, paint shop, sales person, canteen.

The three elements of cost

All costs can be categorised as **labour** or **materials** or **expenses**.

contd

Direct costs

These are costs which can be directly attributed to the making of a particular product, e.g. wood used to make a table. Not only can you identify the wood with a specific product, but you can also measure the exact amount of wood used to make each table and therefore determine its cost. This is an example of **direct materials**.

You can also identify the number of hours it takes a worker to make the table, and, using their rate of pay, determine the labour cost of making the table. This is an example of **direct wages**, also known as **direct labour**.

If the table was being made to a design that had been patented, you may have to pay royalties for each table made. This is known as **direct expenses**. Another common example of direct expenses would be the hire of a special machine for that one job or product.

All the direct costs of a job or service added together make up what is known as the **prime cost** of the job.

Direct materials + Direct labour + Direct expenses = Prime cost.

Indirect costs

These are also commonly known as **overheads**. These costs cannot be directly allocated to a particular product or activity. For example, a factory making 4 different products could not directly attribute the electricity bill to the making of any one product. Other examples of indirect costs could be rent, administration, supervision, canteen or maintenance.

Fixed costs

Fixed costs are those costs which do not vary directly with the level of production, e.g. rent. This means that if a company pays £1,000 a month in rent, the rent will still be £1,000 whether they produce 5,000 products or 10,000 products. In fact, if the factory shuts down for a fortnight at Christmas time and zero products are produced, the rent will still have to be paid.

Variable costs

These are costs which vary directly with the level of production, e.g. direct materials. This means that if the company is making a table that takes 2 square metres of wood, then 10 tables will require 20 square metres and 40 tables will require 80 square metres.

Semi-variable costs

These are costs which have a fixed element as well as a variable element. Power is a good example of this, because an electricity or gas bill will have a standing charge which is the same every month, and then on top of that you pay a usage charge for each unit that you use. Clearly, the more you produce, the longer the machines are running and the more power you are using, so this part of the bill is varying directly with the level of production. Again, the standing charge needs to be paid whether you are using power or not, and so it is classed as 'fixed'.

ONLINE

Find the answers to all of the questions and exercises in this book at www.brightredbooks.net

DON'T FORGET

Management accounting is concerned with collecting high-quality information to aid decision-making.

DON'T FORGET

Direct materials + Direct labour + Direct expenses = Prime cost.

DON'T FORGET

Variable costs vary directly with the level of production, whereas fixed costs vary with time.

ONLINE TEST

Head to www.brightredbooks. net to test yourself on management accounting.

 THINGS TO DO AND THINK ABOUT

1. Describe two duties of the management accountant.
2. Describe two advantages of management accounting.
3. Explain what is meant by the term 'cost centre'.
4. State the three elements of cost.
5. Outline the difference between direct and indirect costs.
6. Explain what is meant by the term 'prime cost'.
7. Outline the difference between fixed and variable costs.

INVENTORY CONTROL

METHODS OF INVENTORY CONTROL

At any given time, a company will hold a certain amount of inventory which may include raw materials, work in progress, finished goods or consumables. Raw materials must be readily available in sufficient quantities in order to ensure that production is not interrupted.

Given that a substantial amount of money is tied up in inventories and that many of the items held can be of a high value, it is necessary to keep a tight control on them to prevent theft and to ensure that items are held under the correct conditions so that they are not damaged or spoiled.

There are many costs involved in holding inventory, including wages for warehouse staff; the cost of keeping the inventory secure; heating; ventilation; insurance and storage space to name but a few.

Inventory is held in a storeroom or warehouse, and specialist personnel are employed to control inventory movement and security. Here, detailed records will be kept of all items. All movements in and out are recorded and levels monitored. Normally each item will be stored in a specific location, known as a bin, and a bin card at the front will record movements in and out of that bin.

Inventory should be regularly counted in order to ensure that all records and valuation of inventories shown in the accounts are accurate. The three main methods of counting inventories are **periodic**, **continuous** and **perpetual inventory**. The main method is **perpetual inventory**.

PRICING OF STORES ISSUES

Anyone requiring materials or goods from the storeroom or warehouse will be required to present a signed requisition from authorised personnel. The warehouse staff will then issue the items and record the issue on the bin card and update the balance. An example of a bin card is shown here.

Part number	A 1234			Bin no./ location	A1284		
Description	30cm brackets						
Receipts			**Issues**				**Balance**
Date	Goods received note number	Quantity	Date	Goods received note number	Quantity		
							b/f 100
15/01/2013	1235	200					300
			29/01/2013	1929	140		160
			03/02/2013	1955	120		20
10/02/2013	1384	500					520

The bin card only shows the amount of items in the bin. The value of the inventory is shown on an inventory record card together with the number of items and their purchase prices, resulting in a valuation of the balance in inventory. A simple example of an inventory record card is shown below.

However, since all inventory items may have been purchased on different dates at different prices, this poses a problem for the costing of the finished product. What if half the parts in a batch are bought at £5 and the other half were bought at £6 each? Do we charge the customer one price for half of their order and another price for the other half? This would be unworkable, and customers would be unlikely to accept multiple prices in one order for identical products.

The problem can be overcome by using a system of perpetual inventory called the **weighted average** method of pricing stores issues. It is also more commonly called the **average cost** and is abbreviated as **AVCO**.

Stock item:	iPad 2	IN			OUT			BALANCE		
Date	Reference	Qty	Cost	Value	Qty	Cost	Value	Qty	Cost	Value
01 Jun	Balance							10	200	2,000
13 Jun	Invoice 46	40	200	8,000				50	200	10,000
15 Jun	Receipt 19				5	200	1,000	45	200	9,000
17 Jun	Receipt 28				7	200	1,400	38	200	7,600
24 Jun	Invoice 47	20	200	4,000				58	200	11,600
29 Jun	Receipt 72				3	200	600	55	200	11,000

contd

Example:

The following receipts and issues relate to part number AB12.

Receipts	Issues
1 Jan Purchased 200 @ £5 each Invoice no. 111	2 Jan Issued 50 items to production Requisition no. 42
4 Jan Purchased 350 @ £6 each Invoice no. 435	5 Jan Issued 50 items to production Requisition no. 43
7 Jan Purchased 200 @ £7 each Invoice no. 874	9 Jan Issued 60 items to production Requisition no. 44

You are required to prepare an inventory record card for the month of June using the average cost (AVCO) method of pricing stores issues.

Step 1 – Enter the receipts and issues for 1 and 2 January as follows:

Part No: AB12		Receipts			Issues			Balance		
Date	Details	Qty	Price	Value	Qty	Price	Value	Qty	Price	Value
1 Jan	Invoice no. 111	200	£5.00	£1,000.00				200	£5.00	£1,000.00
2 Jan	Requisition no. 42				50	£5.00	£250.00	150	£5.00	£750.00

This is quite simple, as we only have 200 units in inventory and they are all priced at £5.00.

Step 2 – Enter the receipt on 4 January and add the quantity to the balance to give a new quantity balance of 500 units. Then add the value to the previous value balance of £750 to give a new balance value of £2,850.

Part No: AB12		Receipts			Issues			Balance		
Date	Details	Qty	Price	Value	Qty	Price	Value	Qty	Price	Value
1 Jan	Invoice no. 111	200	£5.00	£1,000.00				200	£5.00	£1,000.00
2 Jan	Requisition no. 42				50	£5.00	£250.00	150	£5.00	£750.00
4 Jan	Invoice no. 435	350	£6.00	£2,100.00				500		£2,850.00

Now divide the value by the quantity in the balance column to get the new average price per unit, i.e. £2,850 ÷ 500 = £5.70.

NB – A new price is only calculated when a new batch is received with a different price. So, the next requisition on 5 January is issued at the average price of £5.70.

Part No: AB12		Receipts			Issues			Balance		
Date	Details	Qty	Price	Value	Qty	Price	Value	Qty	Price	Value
1 Jan	Invoice no. 111	200	£5.00	£1,000.00				200	£5.00	£1,000.00
2 Jan	Requisition no. 42				50	£5.00	£250.00	150	£5.00	£750.00
4 Jan	Invoice no. 435	350	£6.00	£2,100.00				500	£5.70	£2,850.00
5 Jan	Requisition no. 43				50	£5.70	£285.00	450	£5.70	£2,565.00

Step 3 – Enter the receipt from 7 January and calculate the new average price in the exact same way as we did on 5 January. Then make the issue on 9 January at the new price.

Part No: AB12		Receipts			Issues			Balance		
Date	Details	Qty	Price	Value	Qty	Price	Value	Qty	Price	Value
1 Jan	Invoice no. 111	200	£5.00	£1,000.00				200	£5.00	£1,000.00
2 Jan	Requisition no. 42				50	£5.00	£250.00	150	£5.00	£750.00
4 Jan	Invoice no. 435	350	£6.00	£2,100.00				500	£5.70	£2,850.00
5 Jan	Requisition no. 43				50	£5.70	£285.00	450	£5.70	£2,565.00
7 Jan	Invoice no. 874	200	£7.00	£1,400.00				650	£6.10	£3,965.00
9 Jan	Requisition no. 44				60	£6.10	£366.00	590	£6.10	£3,599.00

The closing inventory valuation on 9 January is £3,599.00.

In this case, the new prices all work out evenly – but it is not unusual to get a rounding error within the calculations. This can be handled by calculating a new average price at the end to get a more even valuation – or, if it is only a couple of pence, it can be ignored.

THINGS TO DO AND THINK ABOUT

1. Explain the AVCO method of pricing stores issues.
2. Describe one advantage and one disadvantage of AVCO.

EXERCISES ON INVENTORY CONTROL

RETURNS

If goods are returned, then they must be returned at their original purchase price so a full refund can be obtained. If, in the above example, we wish to return 90 of the items bought on 4 January, and the fault is not discovered until 10 January, the inventory record card would be updated as follows:

Part No: AB12		Receipts			Issues			Balance		
Date	Details	Qty	Price	Value	Qty	Price	Value	Qty	Price	Value
1 Jan	Invoice no. 111	200	£5.00	£1,000.00				200	£5.00	£1,000.00
2 Jan	Requisition no. 42				50	£5.00	£250.00	150	£5.00	£750.00
4 Jan	Invoice no. 435	350	£6.00	£2,100.00				500	£5.70	£2,850.00
5 Jan	Requisition no. 43				50	£5.70	£285.00	450	£5.70	£2,565.00
7 Jan	Invoice no. 874	200	£7.00	£1,400.00				650	£6.10	£3,965.00
9 Jan	Requisition no. 44				60	£6.10	£366.00	590	£6.10	£3,599.00
10 Jan	Returns				90	£6.00	£540.00	500	£6.12	£3,059.00

Note that a new average price has to be calculated when a return is made. In this case, we were left with 500 items totalling £3,059. When we divide to get a new average price, this gives us an answer of £6.118, which is then rounded to £6.12.

Advantages of AVCO	Disadvantages of AVCO
Items are valued at the same cost even if they are purchased at different prices and/or dates	The average cost may bear no resemblance to the prices actually paid for the items
Closing inventory valuations are fairly close to the current market price	Rounding problems with constantly recalculating average prices increase the risk of errors
The method allows comparisons between profits from different periods	Where prices are rising quickly, the average cost may be lower than the replacement cost
It smooths out price fluctuations	
The method is acceptable to the Inland Revenue	

 EXERCISE 1

The following information relates to the movements of part no. XY26 during the month of February.

Receipts		Issues	
1 Feb	Purchased 1,000 @ £1 each	3 Feb	Issued 500 items to production
	Invoice no. 753		Requisition no. 114
5 Feb	Purchased 500 @ £1.50 each	7 Feb	Issued 250 items to production
	Invoice no. 975		Requisition no. 118
9 Feb	Purchased 1,000 @ £3 each	11 Feb	Issued 100 items to production
	Invoice no. 420		Requisition no. 121

You are required to prepare an inventory record card for the month of February using the average cost (AVCO) method of pricing stores issues.

 EXERCISE 2

The following information relates to the movements of part no. 765 during the month of March.

Receipts		Issues	
8 Mar	Purchased 500 @ £10 each	10 Mar	Issued 250 items to production
	Invoice no. 987		Requisition no. 106
12 Mar	Purchased 750 @ £12 each	14 Mar	Issued 500 items to production
	Invoice no. 921		Requisition no. 125
15 Mar	Purchased 500 @ £12.50 each	19 Mar	Issued 300 items to production
	Invoice no. 1007		Requisition no. 130

You are required to prepare an inventory record card for the month of March using the average cost (AVCO) method of pricing stores issues.

contd

 **EXERCISE 3**

The following information relates to the movements of part no. 446A during the month of April.

Receipts		Issues	
10 Apr	Purchased 500 @ £5 each	12 Apr	Issued 250 items to production
	Invoice no. 212		Requisition no. 246
15 Apr	Purchased 1,000 @ £6 each	18 Apr	Issued 500 items to production
	Invoice no. 547		Requisition no. 249
22 Apr	Purchased 500 @ £8 each	25 Apr	Issued 350 items to production
	Invoice no. 897		Requisition no. 254
28 Apr	Purchased 1,500 @ £9 each	30 Apr	Issued 400 items to production
	Invoice no. 996		Requisition no. 260

You are required to prepare an inventory record card for the month of April using the average cost (AVCO) method of pricing stores issues.

 **EXERCISE 4**

The following information relates to the movements of part no. 33A during the month of January.

Receipts		Issues	
4 Jan	Balance b/f 1,000 @ £15 each	7 Jan	Issued 250 items to production
			Requisition no. 22
9 Jan	Purchased 500 @ £16 each	10 Jan	Returned 500 items bought on 9 Jan
	Invoice no. 731		
14 Jan	Purchased 500 @ £16.50 each	17 Jan	Issued 350 items to production
	Invoice no. 1043		Requisition no. 30
20 Jan	Purchased 1,400 @ £17.10 each	22 Jan	Issued 400 items to production
	Invoice no. 8765		Requisition no. 43

You are required to prepare an inventory record card for the month of January using the average cost (AVCO) method of pricing stores issues.

 **EXERCISE 5**

The following information relates to the movements of part no. PV66 during the month of May.

Receipts		Issues	
1 May	Balance b/f 150 @ £2.50 each	1 May	Issued 100 items to production
			Requisition no. 105
2 May	Purchased 300 @ £3 each	4 May	Issued 100 items to production
	Invoice no. X234		Requisition no. 113
5 May	Purchased 500 @ £3.40 each	7 May	Returned 150 items bought on 2 May
	Invoice no. 7308		
9 May	Purchased 400 @ £3.60 each	12 May	Issued 250 items to production
	Invoice no. 7575		Requisition no. 117
16 May	Purchased 200 @ £3.75 each	14 May	Issued 150 items to production
	Invoice no. 8404		Requisition no. 120

You are required to prepare an inventory record card for the month of May using the average cost (AVCO) method of pricing stores issues.

 **EXERCISE 6**

The following information relates to the movements of part no. 1036 during the month of June.

Receipts		Issues	
4 Jun	Purchased 500 @ £1.50 each	6 Jun	Issued 250 items to production
	Invoice no. 00043		Requisition no. 236
5 Jun	Purchased 750 @ £1.70 each	10 Jun	Issued 300 items to production
	Invoice no. 40065		Requisition no. 240
9 Jun	Purchased 400 @ £2.20 each	14 Jun	Issued 100 items to production
	Invoice no. J654		Requisition no. 245

You are required to prepare an inventory record card for the month of June using the average cost (AVCO) method of pricing stores issues.

 ONLINE

For more exercises on inventory control, head to www.brightredbooks.net

OVERHEAD ANALYSIS 1

WHAT ARE OVERHEADS?

These are the **indirect costs** which are not easily identifiable in a product. However, without these costs, the product could not be made. Overhead analysis is the process of including an amount for each overhead in the product being made or service being provided.

Examples of overheads include:

Rent and rates	Electricity	Insurance
Cleaning expenses	Administration costs	Repairs and maintenance costs

Example:

When examining a cake made in a factory, it is easy to see costs such as the material costs – flour, milk and chocolate – needed for the production of the cake. However, it is not easy to identify costs such as electricity, cleaning costs and the rent of the factory in the cake. Still, the cake could not have been produced in the first place without the business paying for rent and electricity.

Before we look any further at the study of **overheads**, you must understand what is meant by the terms **cost unit** and **cost centre**.

COST UNIT	COST CENTRE
A cost unit is the product or service being manufactured/provided. In simple terms, this is the item which the business is trying to work out the cost of producing. Examples of cost units are: • loaf of bread • carton of soup • meal served in a restaurant • tyre for a car • television set • operation in a hospital • pint of beer	This is simply a department or area of a business where costs can be gathered from or 'charged' to. Indeed, your school uses cost centres as a way of working out the cost of running the school. Typical cost centres in a school could be: • English Department • Maths Department • ICT Department • School office • School canteen • Janitorial and cleaning • School library The costs gathered from each cost centre can then be added to work out the total cost of running the school.

Referring back to the example above about producing cakes (the **cost unit**), typical **cost centres** in a factory could be:

- mixing
- firing
- decorating
- packaging
- storage
- office and administration.

Again, the costs gathered from each cost centre can then be added to work out the total cost of operating the factory.

There are two main types of cost centre:

1. Production
2. Service.

Production cost centres

Production cost centres are those departments which are directly engaged in the process of production of goods or delivery of a service. Typical examples include machining or assembly cost centres.

Service cost centres

Service cost centres are those departments which are not directly involved in the production process but provide services to the production cost centres, for example cleaning and maintenance, or stores departments.

contd

Example:

A paint manufacturer has the following cost centres: Mixing Department, Packaging Department, Stores Department, Maintenance Department and Staff Canteen. The Mixing and Packaging Departments are **production cost centres**, as they are **directly** involved in producing the paint and making it ready for sale. Stores, Maintenance and Canteen are **service cost centres**, as they are **not directly** involved in producing paint. Instead, they provide additional services to the production cost centres.

Allocation of overheads

This refers to the allotment of whole items of overhead costs to cost centres; that is, overhead costs can be allotted **directly** to a cost centre. For example, if the canteen is treated as a separate cost centre, then the wages of the canteen manager are allocated to that cost centre.

Indirect labour and indirect materials are usually able to be allocated directly to cost centres.

Apportionment of overheads

This is where overhead costs are shared out among various cost centres on some fair and equitable basis, since the overhead cannot be directly allocated to any one particular cost centre. For example, rent and rates cannot be allocated to any particular cost centre and so must be apportioned (shared) amongst all cost centres in the business.

Apportionment of overheads to cost centres

Unallocated overhead costs must be apportioned (divided) to the various cost centres in a way that reflects the benefits that individual cost centres receive from the overhead cost. For example, the rent of a factory will be divided between all cost centres in the factory according to the area occupied by each cost centre. As such, it is fair that those cost centres with more space will be charged with a greater share of the rent.

Some of the more common bases used for apportionment of overheads to cost centres are as follows:

OVERHEAD COST	BASIS OF APPORTIONMENT
Rent, rates, heat and light, building expenses, property insurance and cleaning	Floor area occupied by each cost centre
Depreciation of plant and machinery and insurance of machinery	Book value of the non-current asset
Human resource and welfare costs, canteen costs, administration costs	Number of employees
Electricity, gas and water charges	Metered consumption
Power	Kilowatt hours

Any business is unlikely to know what their exact overheads will be until the end of their financial year, when all overhead costs will have been identified and totalled. However, it is necessary to work out the cost of producing each cost unit in order to determine a selling price. As such, businesses will use **estimated** or **budgeted** overhead costs. Estimated or budgeted overheads will be based on historical accounting information and past business experience.

THINGS TO DO AND THINK ABOUT

Answer the following questions in your workbook.

1. Explain, using appropriate examples, the difference between direct and indirect costs.
2. Explain what is meant by a cost unit and a cost centre.
3. Describe the difference between a production cost centre and a service cost centre.
4. State two indirect costs that can be allocated directly to cost centres.
5. Outline what is meant by apportionment of overheads.
6. Describe some of the bases that could be used to apportion overheads to cost centres.
7. Explain why it may be necessary for a business to use budgeted overheads when undertaking overhead analysis.

DON'T FORGET

'Allocated' means that an overhead cost can be charged directly to a cost centre.

DON'T FORGET

Apportionment means that an overhead cost has to be shared among various cost centres.

DON'T FORGET

A business will use budgeted/estimated overheads to undertake overhead apportionment.

ONLINE

Head to www.brightredbooks.net for exercises on overheads.

ONLINE TEST

Test yourself on overheads at www.brightredbooks.net

OVERHEAD ANALYSIS 2

PREPARATION OF OVERHEAD ANALYSIS STATEMENTS

Example:

Cakes for all Occasions operate a factory in Glasgow and provide you with the following information for Year 2 relating to five cost centres – **three production** and **two service**.

	Baking	Decorating	Packaging	Maintenance	Stores	Total
Floor area (m²)	20,000	10,000	15,000	2,500	2,500	50,000
Machinery (cost)	£80,000	£20,000	£50,000	£30,000	£20,000	£200,000
Employees	10	25	10	3	2	50
kW hours	200,000	150,000	50,000	60,000	40,000	500,000
Indirect materials	£80,500	£25,000	£15,250	£4,500	£2,500	£127,750

Estimated overheads to be **apportioned** in Year 2 are as follows:

Overhead	Amount	Basis of apportionment
Rent	£100,000	Floor area
Depreciation of machinery	£20,000	Cost of machinery
Supervision	£60,000	Employees
Heat and light	£120,000	Floor area
Power	£80,000	kW hours
Indirect materials	£127,750	

Solution:

OVERHEAD ANALYSIS STATEMENT								
Overhead iem	Basis of apportionment	Total	Rate	Production cost centres			Service cost centres	
				Baking	Decorating	Packaging	Maintenance	Stores
Indirect materials	**Allocated**	£127,750		£80,500	£25,000	£15,250	£4,500	£2,500
Rent	Floor area	£100,000	£2.00	£40,000	£20,000	£30,000	£5,000	£5,000
Depreciation of machinery	Value of machinery	£20,000	£0.10	£8,000	£2,000	£5,000	£3,000	£2,000
Supervision	Employees	£60,000	£1,200	£12,000	£30,000	£12,000	£3,600	£2,400
Heat and light	Floor area	£120,000	£2.40	£48,000	£24,000	£36,000	£6,000	£6,000
Power	kW hours	£80,000	£0.16	£32,000	£24,000	£8,000	£9,600	£6,400
Total cost-centre overheads				**£220,500**	**£125,000**	**£106,250**	**£31,700**	**£24,300**

Notes
1. Indirect materials have been **ALLOCATED** and so can be charged directly to specific cost centres.
2. **Apportionment rates** are calculated by dividing the total estimated overhead by the total of the relevant basis of apportionment. For example, the rate for rent is calculated by dividing £100,000 by the floor area of 50,000 m². The rate for depreciation of machinery is calculated by dividing £20,000 by the value of machinery, £200,000 and so on.

VIDEO LINK

To see more on overhead apportionment, go online and watch the video at www.brightredbooks.net

DON'T FORGET

Service cost-centre overheads are reapportioned to production cost centres.

REAPPORTIONMENT OF SERVICE COST CENTRES

The final stage in the apportionment of overhead costs is to apportion the **service cost centre** overheads onto the **production cost centres** on some suitable basis that reflects the usage of the service cost centres by the production cost centres.

Worked example

Below is an extract from an overhead analysis schedule from Young's Ltd showing the overheads apportioned to each cost centre for Year 2.

contd

OVERHEAD ANALYSIS STATEMENT

Overhead item	Basis of apportionment	Total	Rate	Production cost centres			Service cost centres	
				Spinning	Dyeing	Weaving	Canteen	Stores
Total cost-centre overheads				£400,500	£250,000	£150,000	£55,000	£40,000

Additional information:

	Spinning	Dyeing	Weaving	Canteen	Stores	Total
Labour hours	220,000	90,000	60,000	30,000	50,000	450,000
Number of employees	35	30	15	25	10	115

Service cost-centre overheads are to be reapportioned to production and service cost centres in the following order:

- Stores first on the basis of labour hours
- Canteen on the basis of number of employees.

Solution:

OVERHEAD ANALYSIS STATEMENT

Overhead item	Basis of apportionment	Total	Rate	Production cost centres			Service cost centres	
				Spinning	Dyeing	Weaving	Canteen	Stores
Total cost-centre overheads				£400,500	£250,000	£150,000	£55,000	£40,000
Stores	Labour hours	£40,000	£0.10	£22,000	£9,000	£6,000	£3,000	–
							£58,000	
Canteen	Number of employees	£58,000	£725	£25,375	£21,750	£10,875	–	
Total production cost-centre overheads				£447,875	£280,750	£166,875		

Notes
1. The rate for Stores is calculated as follows:
   £40,000/(220,000 hrs + 90,000 hrs + 60,000 hrs + 30,000 hrs) = £0.10 per labour hour.
2. The Canteen overhead has now increased to £58,000, and it is this figure that must be reapportioned.
3. The rate for Canteen is calculated as follows:
   £58,000/(35 employees + 30 employees + 15 employees) = £725 per employee.

 **DON'T FORGET**

Only the labour hours or number of employees from those cost centres sharing the overhead will be used in the reapportionment.

 THINGS TO DO AND THINK ABOUT

A company has three departments, A, B and C, which have costs apportioned among them on a suitable basis.

The estimated overhead costs for Year 2 are as follows:

Rent	£1,000	Lighting and heating	£100	Canteen expenses	£200
Supervision	£1,500	Depreciation of plant	£400	Rates	£600

	Department A	Department B	Department C	Total
Area (m²)	2,000	1,000	1,000	4,000
No. of employees	25	15	10	50
Value of plant	£10,000	£6,000	£4,000	£20,000

Apportion the overhead costs to each department on a suitable basis.

 **ONLINE TEST**

Test yourself on overheads at www.brightredbooks.net

OVERHEAD ANALYSIS 3

DON'T FORGET

Overhead absorption is the process of charging production cost-centre overheads to cost units.

OVERHEAD ABSORPTION

The stage has now been reached where all the budgeted overheads have been apportioned to the production cost centres, and the task now is to find some suitable basis for charging the production cost centre overheads onto the **cost units** – that is, onto the final products being produced.

The technical term used for this process of charging production overheads onto cost units is known as **overhead absorption** or **overhead recovery**. The table below outlines the most commonly used bases for absorbing overheads from production cost centres to cost units.

RATE PER UNIT PRODUCED With this method, we take the total overheads for the cost centre (department) and divide them by the number of units the cost centre or department is expected to produce. This then gives an overhead charge for each unit produced.	Formula = $\dfrac{\text{Total overheads}}{\text{Total units produced}}$ **Example** $\dfrac{£20,000}{60,000 \text{ units}}$ = 33p per unit
MACHINE-HOUR RATE With this method, we take the total overheads for the cost centre (department) and divide them by the total number of machine hours the cost centre or department is expected to use throughout the year. This then gives an overhead charge for each machine hour spent making the cost unit (or product).	Formula = $\dfrac{\text{Total overheads}}{\text{Total machine hours used}}$ **Example** $\dfrac{£80,000}{20,000 \text{ machine hours}}$ = £4 per machine hour
DIRECT LABOUR-HOUR RATE With this method, we take the total overheads for the cost centre (department) and divide them by the total number of direct labour hours the cost centre or department is expected to use throughout the year. This then gives an overhead charge for each labour hour spent making the cost unit or product.	Formula = $\dfrac{\text{Total overheads}}{\text{Total labour hours used}}$ **Example** $\dfrac{£120,000}{60,000 \text{ labour hours}}$ = £2 per labour hour
PERCENTAGE OF DIRECT WAGES With this method, we determine a percentage that will be applied to all cost units based on the direct wage cost. For example, overheads will be charged to each cost unit based on 50% of the direct wage cost used to produce each unit.	Formula = $\dfrac{\text{Cost-centre overheads}}{\text{Cost of direct wages}} \times 100$ $\dfrac{£75,000}{£150,000} \times 100$ = 50% of direct wage cost
PERCENTAGE OF DIRECT MATERIALS With this method, we determine a percentage that will be applied to all cost units based on the direct material cost. For example, overheads will be charged to each cost unit based on 50% of the direct material cost used to produce each unit.	Formula = $\dfrac{\text{Cost-centre overheads}}{\text{Cost of direct materials}} \times 100$ $\dfrac{£250,000}{£500,000} \times 100$ = 50% of direct materials cost
PERCENTAGE OF PRIME COSTS With this method, we determine a percentage that will be applied to all cost units based on the prime cost (direct labour + direct materials) used to produce each cost unit. For example, overheads will be charged to each cost unit based on 50% of the prime cost used to produce each unit.	Formula = $\dfrac{\text{Cost-centre overheads}}{\text{Total prime cost}} \times 100$ $\dfrac{£50,000}{£100,000} \times 100$ = 50% of prime cost

Example:

Here are the budgeted/estimated production cost-centre overheads for Young's Ltd

Young's Ltd – Year 2	Spinning	Dyeing	Weaving
Production cost-centre overheads	£	£	£
	447,875	280,750	166,875

contd

The following budgeted information is also available for each production cost centre.

	Spinning	Dyeing	Weaving
Machine hours	100,000	180,000	60,000
Labour hours	120,000	200,000	80,000
Units produced			90,000

Overheads are to be **absorbed** into production using the following bases:
- Spinning – machine hours
- Dyeing – labour hours
- Weaving – units produced.

Show the overhead absorption rates for each production cost centre correct to 2 decimal places.

Solution:

Spinning	Dyeing	Weaving
Overheads = £447,875 Machine hours = 100,000 Rate = £447,875/100,000 = **£4.48 per machine hour**	Overheads = £280,750 Labour hours = 200,000 Rate = £280,750/200,000 = **£1.40 per labour hour**	Overheads = £166,875 Units produced = 90,000 Rate = £166,875/90,000 = **£1.85 per unit**

OVER- AND UNDER-ABSORPTION OF OVERHEADS

As estimated overheads have been used, it is likely that when we come to the end of the accounting period the actual overhead costs incurred will differ from the overheads absorbed into the cost units.

If the **actual overheads** for the accounting period are **greater than** the **overheads absorbed**, then the business will have **underabsorbed costs** and so will have to charge this 'loss' to the Income Statement as an expense.

Cost centre A		
	Budgeted data	**Actual data**
Overheads	£50,000	£52,000
Direct labour hours	5,000 hours	5,050 hours

1. Direct labour hour rate = (Budgeted overheads/Budgeted hours)
   £50,000/5,000 hours = £10 per hour.
2. Overhead absorbed = (Actual direct labour hours x Overhead absorption rate) 5,050 hours x £10 = £50,500.
3. **Overheads underabsorbed** = (Actual overhead – Absorbed overhead) £52,000 – £50,500 = £1,500.
4. £1,500 would be recorded as an expense in the Income Statement.

On the other hand, if the **actual overheads** for the accounting period are **less than** the **overheads absorbed**, then the business will have **overabsorbed** costs and will record this 'gain' under other income in the Income Statement.

Cost centre A		
	Budgeted data	**Actual data**
Overheads	£50,000	£49,400
Direct labour hours	5,000 hours	4,950 hours

1. Direct labour hour rate = (Budgeted overheads/Budgeted hours)
   £50,000/5,000 hours = £10 per hour.
2. Overheads absorbed = (Actual direct labour hours x Overhead absorption rate) 4,950 hours x £10 = £49,500
3. **Overheads overabsorbed** = (Actual overhead – Absorbed overhead) £49,500 – £49,400 = £100
4. £100 would be recorded as a gain in the Income Statement.

FACTORY-WIDE OVERHEAD ABSORPTION RATES

It may be the case that the cost accountant decides that it is fairer and simpler to have a factory-wide overhead absorption rate which is applied to all cost centres, rather than separate cost centre overhead absorption rates. However, this makes no allowances for the fact that different cost centres use up overheads at different rates.

DON'T FORGET

Absorption rates are usually calculated to 2 decimal places.

DON'T FORGET

When actual overheads are greater than overheads absorbed, the business will have underabsorbed overheads.

DON'T FORGET

When actual overheads are less than overheads absorbed, the business will have overabsorbed overheads.

DON'T FORGET

A factory-wide absorption rate is a single rate applied to all cost centres.

ONLINE

Head to www.brightredbooks.net to find the answers to all questions and exercises in this book.

ONLINE TEST

Test yourself on overheads at www.brightredbooks.net

EXERCISES ON OVERHEAD ANALYSIS 1

 EXERCISE 1

Bryson Ltd has two production cost centres A and B and two service cost centres C and D. The following information is available for each department.

	Production		Service		
	A	**B**	**C**	**D**	**Total**
Indirect labour	£15,000	£18,000	£8,000	£4,000	£45,000
Floor area (sq m)	20,000	8,000	6,000	6,000	40,000
Cost of equipment	£70,000	£80,000	£30,000	£20,000	£200,000
Number of employees	15	30	5	10	60

The following overhead costs are to be apportioned to the above departments:

Overhead	Amount	Basis of apportionment
Rates	£8,000	Floor area
Depreciation of equipment	£20,000	Cost of equipment
Supervision	£30,000	No. of employees
Insurance of premises	£60,000	Floor area

Prepare an overhead analysis statement.

EXERCISE 2

Higgins plc has two production cost centres E and F and two service cost centres G and H. The following information is available for each cost centre.

	E	**F**	**G**	**H**	**Total**
Indirect labour	£20,000	£18,000	£25,000	£22,000	£85,000
Floor area (sq m)	30,000	25,000	15,000	20,000	90,000
Value of equipment (cost)	£60,000	£50,000	£40,000	£60,000	£210,000
Employees	20	30	20	25	95
Machine hours	20,000	15,000	5,000	10,000	50,000

The following overhead costs are to be apportioned to the above cost centres.

Power	£40,000	Machine hours
Supervision	£9,500	Number of employees
Rates	£45,000	Floor area
Heat and light	£18,000	Floor area
Maintenance of machinery	£6,000	Machine hours
Depreciation	10% of cost	Value of equipment (cost)

Prepare an overhead analysis statement.

contd

⚙ EXERCISE 3

The Pre-Aft Manufacturing Company has two production and two service departments. The factory overhead expenses incurred for the month of August Year 2 were as follows:

| | Production cost centres | | Service cost centres | |
	Mixing	Packaging	Maintenance	Personnel
Indirect labour	£18,750	£9,360	£8,700	£900
Indirect materials	£6,540	£5,620	£2,600	£350
Electricity	£4,110	£2,750	£3,400	£250
TOTAL	£29,400	£18,000	£14,700	£1,500
Bases for distribution				
No. of employees	53	27	20	
Maintenance labour hours	17	8		

Prepare a distribution of service cost-centre overheads to production departments.

The Personnel cost centre serves the other three departments and should be apportioned first on the basis of the number of employees. The Maintenance cost centre serves the Production cost centres only.

THINGS TO DO AND THINK ABOUT

Exam-style question

The following budgeted data relates to Marquis Ltd, which has three production departments and one service department. The company aimed to produce 10,000 units during the period represented by this data.

On the overhead analysis sheet provided for this question, you are required to:

| | Production Depts | | | Service Dept |
	Mixing	Firing	Finishing	Maintenance
Area (sq m)	2,000	1,800	2,680	1,520
No. of employees	42	36	28	14
Metered (kW hours)	1,000	1,000	1,200	800
Machinery cost	£80,000	£40,000	£60,000	£20,000
Estimated machine hours	8,000	6,000	4,000	–
Estimated labour hours	–	4,000	8,000	

Overheads	Total cost
Factory administration	£120,000
Heating and lighting	£10,000
Depreciation	20% of machinery cost
Power	£40,000

1. Show the overhead apportioned to each departmental cost centre.
2. Reapportion the total overhead cost of the service department to the production department on the basis of machine hours worked.
3. Calculate, to the **nearest whole pound**, the overhead recovery rate for each of the production departments on the following basis:
    Mixing department – machine hours
    Firing department – labour hours
    Finishing department – number of units produced
4. The actual accounting data for the period was as follows:

	Mixing	Firing	Finishing
Overheads	£85,000	£64,500	£60,200
Machine hours	8,200		
Labour hours		4,200	
Units produced			9,800

Calculate overheads over- or underabsorbed in each cost centre.

EXERCISES ON OVERHEAD ANALYSIS 2

EXERCISE 1

The Tayforth Company Ltd has 3 service departments – Buildings, Maintenance and Canteen – and 4 production departments – Cutting, Turning, Assembly and Painting.

The departmental overhead expenses for the month of October Year 2 were:

Buildings £7,750	Cutting £6,000	Painting £5,850	Assembly £9,850
Maintenance £8,150	Turning £6,450	Canteen £4,050	

The overheads of service departments are distributed in the following manner, and in the following order:

1. Costs of Buildings on the basis of total wages, which were: Maintenance £3,200, Turning £30,200, Canteen £1,400, Assembly £18,400, Cutting £10,200 and Painting £14,100.
2. Costs of Maintenance on a percentage basis: Canteen 5%, Turning 8%, Painting 60%, Cutting 12% and Assembly 15%.
3. Costs of Canteen in proportion to number of employees: Cutting 220, Turning 964, Assembly 360 and Painting 300.

Show the distribution of service-department costs.

EXERCISE 2

The following overheads have been apportioned to the cost centres in Smiths Ltd.

	Production departments		Service departments	
	Binding	Packaging	Personnel	Maintenance
Departmental overheads	£85,000	£60,000	£30,000	£55,000

Additional information:

	Binding	Packaging	Personnel	Maintenance
Number of employees	30	20	10	10
Machine hours	10,000	5,000		

You are required to reapportion the service cost centre overheads on the following basis:

1. Personnel overheads first on the basis of the number of employees in each department.
2. Maintenance costs on the basis of machine hours.

EXERCISE 3

Grant and McCallum are in partnership and provide you with the apportioned overhead costs for each of their 2 production cost centres:

	Cost centre A	Cost centre B	Total
Budgeted overheads	£9,000	£4,000	£13,000

Overheads are absorbed on the basis of direct labour hours in cost centre A and machine hours in cost centre B. The following information is also available:

contd

	Cost centre A	Cost centre B
Total direct labour hours	4,000	
Total direct machine hours		5,000

Calculate the absorption rate for each cost centre, correct to 2 decimal places.

 EXERCISE 4

Calculate the overhead absorption rates (correct to 2 decimal places) for each of the following production cost centres using the basis given.

Dundee factory

Production cost centre	Overhead	Basis of absorption
Cutting	£350,000	100,000 direct labour hours
Filling	£210,000	£70,000 prime cost
Assembly	£90,000	£22,500 direct materials cost

 EXERCISE 5

Calculate the overhead absorption rates (correct to 2 decimal places) for each of the following production cost centres using the basis given.

Aberdeen factory

Production cost centre	Overhead	Basis of absorption
Cost centre 1	£350,000	100,000 direct labour hours
Cost centre 2	£140,000	£35,000 direct materials cost
Cost centre 3	£160,000	40,000 direct labour hours

 EXERCISE 6

The following information relates to cost centre B, where overheads are absorbed on the basis of machine hours.

Cost centre B		
	Budgeted data	**Actual data**
Overheads	£60,000	£58,000
Machine hours	10,000 hours	9,600 hours

You are required to calculate the following:

1. Absorption rate for cost centre B
2. Total overheads absorbed
3. Overheads over- or underabsorbed.

 EXERCISE 7

The following information relates to cost centre C, where overheads are absorbed on the basis of machine hours.

Cost centre C		
	Budgeted data	**Actual data**
Overheads	£45,000	£46,200
Direct labour hours	9,000 hours	9,500 hours

You are required to calculate the following:

1. Absorption rate for cost centre C
2. Total overheads absorbed
3. Overheads over- or underabsorbed.

JOB COSTING

JOB-COSTING SYSTEMS

Job costing is used in businesses which perform work on specific jobs, orders or contracts which can be identified throughout the various stages of production. A job-costing system is one in which the costs incurred are allocated or apportioned to the job (which is the cost centre). Job costing is used in connection with:

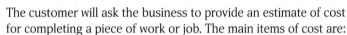

- garages – repairing a motor car
- landscaping – designing and creating a garden
- construction – building a house or even designing and installing a bathroom or kitchen
- fashion – designing and creating a wedding dress.

Each job is manufactured or carried out to the customer's requirements. It is also widely used for the costing of **batches** of similar articles such as shoes or nuts and bolts.

The main purpose of job costing is to determine the profit or loss made on each job. This serves as a check on the accuracy of the estimate or comparison with the cost of similar jobs completed in the past, and helps to bring to light any inefficiencies that have occurred in the course of production. Thus job costing separates **profitable** jobs from **unprofitable** ones and provides a check on past estimates as well as a basis for estimating for similar 'jobs' in the future.

Job cost card		Job no.	456
Name of customer: Mrs E. Brogan			Total cost
MATERIALS			
Quantity	Price per unit	Cost	
10 of material X	£50	£500	
6 of material Y	£100	£600	£1,100
LABOUR			
Hours	Rate per hour	Cost	
100	£10	£1,000	£1,000
OTHER DIRECT COSTS			
Hire of a special machine to complete job			£500
PRIME COSTS			£2,600
OVERHEADS	Absorption rate	Cost	
Machining Dept – 60 hours	£1.80	£108	
Finishing Dept – 20 hours	£1.60	£32	£140
Selling and distribution costs			£50
Administration			£20
TOTAL COSTS			£2,810
PROFIT (20%)			£562
CHARGE TO CUSTOMER			£3,372

The customer will ask the business to provide an estimate of cost for completing a piece of work or job. The main items of cost are:

- **Material** – materials can be costed very accurately to each job. Materials are issued on a LIFO (last in first out), a FIFO (first in first out) or an AVCO basis to each job. Only materials which are **direct** in relation to the cost unit (job) are charged in this manner. **Indirect** materials are analysed and accumulated under overhead expenses.
- **Labour** – as jobs are all unique and specific to an individual customer's requirements, an approximate charge for labour can be given. **Direct** labour entries shown on individual time sheets must be analysed by job number and the totals charged to individual jobs. Only wages which are **direct** in relation to the cost unit (job) are posted in this manner. **Indirect** wages are analysed and accumulated as an overhead expense.
- **Overheads** – a charge for overheads will be absorbed onto each job using one of the pre-determined overhead absorption rates looked at earlier, such as machine-hour rate or labour-hour rate.
- **Selling and distribution overheads** – a share of these costs will also be charged to each job.

Job costing brings together the three main elements of cost:

MATERIALS + LABOUR + OVERHEADS

To keep a record of all costs in completing a specific job for a customer, a job cost card/sheet will be used. An example of a job cost sheet is shown here.

PROFIT

Profit can be expressed in two ways:

- mark-up
- profit margin.

Using the mark-up method, a percentage is added to the **cost of a job**. Therefore profit equals:

mark-up % × cost of job.

> **Example:**
>
> If a job costs £5,000 and there is a mark-up of 20%, profit would be (£5,000 × 20% =) £1,000, making the charge to the customer £6,000.

Using the profit margin, profit is expressed as a fraction or percentage of the **selling price**. Selling price is always expressed as 100%.

> **Example:**
>
> If a job costs £5,000 and there has to be a profit margin of 20%, profit would be calculated as follows:
> Selling price = 100%
> Profit margin = 20%
> Cost of job = 80%
> (£5,000/80%) × 100% = £6,250
> Selling price is therefore £6,250 and profit equals (£6,250 – £5,000) £1,250.

 **EXERCISE 1**

Bannerman Ltd uses a mark-up of 25% to the cost of each job. Calculate the profit and the selling price of each of the following jobs:

Job no.	Cost
100	£600
101	£460
102	£700
103	£900

 **EXERCISE 2**

Cahill and Scott are in partnership, and profit is calculated using a profit margin of 25% on each job completed in their factory. Calculate the profit and cost for each of the following:

Job no.	Cost price
104	£3,000
105	£12,000
106	£9,000
107	£6,000

 ## THINGS TO DO AND THINK ABOUT

Short-answer questions

1. Describe what is meant by a job-costing system.
2. Outline types of work where job costing would be used.
3. List the three main elements of cost used in job costing.
4. Explain the two main methods that can be used to calculate profit on specific jobs.
5. Name the document used to record the details of each job.

Specimen exam-style question

Morin and Wingate are in partnership and have been asked to give a quotation for a new job. The job will be completed in their factory, which has two cost centres – Construction and Finishing. Estimated costs for the job are:

Direct materials required £192

Direct labour £488

Total labour hours 20 (12 hours in Construction and 8 hours in Finishing)

Total machine hours 10 (6 hours in Construction and 4 hours in Finishing)

Overheads are charged to jobs as follows:

Construction – £10 per labour hour

Finishing – £25 per machine hour

Morin and Wingate aim to earn a profit margin of 25% on selling price.

Prepare a job-cost statement for the above job showing the price to be charged to the customer.

 DON'T FORGET

The mark-up method of calculating profit adds a percentage to the cost of the job.

 DON'T FORGET

When profit is expressed as a percentage of selling price, this is known as the profit-margin method.

 ONLINE

Find further exercises on job costing at www.brightredbooks.net

 ONLINE TEST

Test yourself on job costing at www.brightredbooks.net

SERVICE COSTING

DON'T FORGET

Service costing is concerned with providing services rather than products. Service costing can also be referred to as operating costing.

DON'T FORGET

Service costing is used to make a decision on mark-up and a charge for the service.

DON'T FORGET

The costs of delivering a service are similar to the costs of making a product.

DON'T FORGET

The main cost in delivering any service is usually labour.

DON'T FORGET

Pay attention to time periods such as per quarter or per month.

DON'T FORGET

When answering exam questions, always lay out your answer in the form of a statement.

ONLINE

Find more exercises on service costing at www.brightredbooks.net

SERVICE (OR OPERATING) COSTING

Job and process costing are methods of product costing and are concerned with manufacturing processes, whereas **service costing** is concerned with providing services. Service costing is sometimes also referred to as **operating costing**.

It will be used by businesses such as hairdressers, taxi companies, bus companies, rail transport, hospitals, dentists, utility companies, haulage and freight companies etc.

The main purpose of service costing is to:

1. ascertain the cost of providing the service in order to control costs and make decisions regarding how to improve the service and make it more effective and efficient

2. compare the cost of providing the service with other financial periods and other similar companies

3. compare the cost of operating the service as opposed to contracting it out

4. make decisions on what price to charge for the service

5. determine the profitability of a particular service.

Normally, a pre-determined cost of providing the service will be worked out for the financial period, and a cost per unit of measure will be determined. This will then be used to make a decision on mark-up and a charge for the service. For example, a taxi company may work out the cost per passenger mile, then add their mark-up for profit – and this will then result in the fare charged per passenger mile. Other examples of service costs and charges include:

Type of service	Costs	Charges
Taxi Bus Train	Cost per passenger mile	Fare per passenger mile
Hospital	Cost per patient hour or day/night	Price per patient hour, day/night
Doctor	Cost per consultation hour (or half-hour)	Charge per hour or half-hour
Hairdresser	Cost per customer Cost per chair per hour	Charge per customer Charge per chair per hour
Solicitors Accountants	Cost per hour	Fee per hour
Haulage company	Cost per tonne-mile	Charge per tonne-mile

COSTS INVOLVED IN RUNNING A SERVICE

The costs of delivering a service are similar to the costs of making a product. They can still be classified into direct and indirect costs as well as fixed and variable costs.

The main cost in delivering any service is usually labour – and this can be direct or indirect labour. For example, a taxi company will have taxi drivers who are directly delivering the service, but it will also have administration workers, cleaners and radio controllers. Therefore, the driver costs will be variable but administration salaries are likely to be fixed.

There will be a number of other costs involved, such as: fuel, premises, taxi licences, road tax, insurance, taxi cleaning, cleaning of office premises, administration, electricity etc., as well as depreciation of the vehicles.

contd

Example:

Lawrie's Lorries is a distribution company which delivers goods from national retailers to customers across Scotland. They have a fleet of 4 lorries which cost £29,000 each and after 5 years will have an estimated resale value of £4,000 each. It is also estimated that each lorry will cover a distance of 200 miles a day over a 5-day week, and half of that on a Saturday shift, and will operate 48 weeks a year.

The annual running costs are as follows:

Drivers' wages – each driver normally works an 8-hour shift for 5 days a week at an hourly rate of £16 per hour and an extra half-shift on Saturday at an overtime rate of time and a half. Each driver works 48 weeks and receives 4 weeks' holiday pay at £640 per week.

Diesel – fuel consumption of each lorry is 12 miles per litre at a cost of £1.05 per litre.

Servicing – each lorry is serviced every 20,000 miles at a cost of £250 per service.

Tyres – a full set of tyres is replaced every 30,000 miles and costs £800 per set.

Insurance – £714 per lorry per year.

Road tax – £650 per lorry per year.

In addition, the company incurs administration and marketing costs which amount to £3,500 per quarter.

You are required to calculate:

1. how many miles each lorry travels per annum;
2. the total cost of operating each lorry per annum;
3. the total annual operating cost of operating the fleet;
4. the cost per mile;
5. the delivery charge per mile if the mark-up is 20%.

Solution:

Miles travelled per lorry per year

200 miles per day x 5 days = 1,000
Add Saturday 100 miles = 1,100 miles per lorry per week
1,100 miles x 48 weeks = 52,800 miles per lorry per year

Total cost of operating each lorry per annum

Start the solution by working out the annual depreciation, then go through all the costs listed one by one, remembering to multiply or divide by 4 lorries/drivers where appropriate and be mindful of time periods such as per quarter or per month.

Note that the workings alongside, while containing all the answers you need, are not the answer to the question. It is necessary to prepare a statement showing all the costs with a total operating cost at the bottom, as follows:

Lawrie's Lorries
TOTAL COST OF OPERATING EACH LORRY PER ANNUM

	£
Depreciation	5,000
Drivers' wages	38,888
Diesel	4,620
Servicing	660
Tyres	1,408
Insurance	714
Road tax	650
Admin and marketing	3,500
	£55,440

Total annual operating cost of the fleet

This is just the cost per lorry multiplied by four, i.e. £55,440 x 4 = £221,760

The cost per mile

This can be worked out by using either the figures for one lorry or the total for 4 lorries, i.e. £55,440 ÷ 52,800 miles = £1.05 per mile

Delivery charge per mile

Cost per mile	£1.05
Add mark-up 20%	£0.21
Charge per mile	£1.26

Working for 1 lorry per year	Total for 4 lorries/ drivers
Depreciation Cost per lorry – £29,000 Years of useful life – 5 years Less residual value – £4,000 Depreciation = £25,000 ÷ 5 = **£5,000 per lorry per year**	£20,000
Drivers' wages Annual wages for 1 driver = 8 hrs x 5 days = 40 hrs per week + overtime 4 hrs x 1.5 = 6 hrs for a Saturday = 40 + 6 = 46 hrs per week x £16 per hour = £736 per week x 48 weeks = £35,328 per year Add holiday pay = 4 weeks x £640 per week = £2,560 **Therefore total annual pay per driver = £36,328 + £2,560 = £38,888**	£155,552
Diesel ÷ 12 = 4,400 litres of fuel a year x £1.05 per litre = **£4,620 per lorry per year**	£18,480
Servicing 52,800 ÷ 20,000 = 2.64 services per annum per lorry x £250 = **£660 per lorry per year**	£2,640
Tyres 52,800 ÷ 30,000 = 1.76 sets of tyres per annum per lorry x £800 = £**1,408 per lorry per year**	£5,632
Insurance £714 per lorry per year	£2,632
Road tax £650 per lorry per year	£2,600
Admin and marketing £2,500 per quarter x 4 = £10,000 per annum ÷ 4 = **£2,500 per lorry per year**	£10,000

THINGS TO DO AND THINK ABOUT

1. Outline the main differences between product costing and service costing.
2. Describe the main purposes of service costing.
3. Describe one fixed cost and one variable cost incurred by a transport company.
4. Explain the steps that would be undertaken to work out the total labour costs of running a service.
5. Describe how the annual costs of tyres and fuel are worked out for a long-distance lorry.
6. Explain how a dentist would work out how much to charge patients.

 ONLINE TEST

Test yourself on service costing at www.brightredbooks.net

EXERCISES ON SERVICE COSTING

 **EXERCISE 1**

M. Roberts is a dental surgeon who is thinking of starting his own private practice with his partner. The firm will consist of two dentists who will each work 35 hours per week (Monday to Friday) for 48 weeks per annum.

The following additional information is available:

1. The equipment for the 2 surgeries has been purchased at a total cost of £50,000. It is expected to last for 8 years and to have a residual value of £10,000.
2. The premises will be rented for £2,000 per month.
3. The firm will employ 2 dental nurses and 1 receptionist. The nurses will each receive an annual salary of £18,000, and the receptionist will receive an annual salary of £14,000.
4. A locum dentist will be employed by each dentist during their 4 weeks' holiday at a cost of £500 per day.
5. Insurance costs will amount to £6,500 per annum.
6. Laboratory fees for the practice will cost £30,000 per annum.
7. Consumable supplies for the practice will cost £22,000 per annum.
8. Office expenses will amount to £5,000.
9. Other expenses will amount to £1,500.

You are required to:

1. prepare a statement to show the annual cost of operating the practice;
2. calculate the total amount each dentist needs to charge per hour achieve a target annual income of £100,000 each.

 **EXERCISE 2**

The Springburn Lawn Tennis club owns 4 tennis courts, which it rents out to members of the public for an hourly charge which includes the hire of 2 racquets and a tennis ball. The courts are open for a total of 30 weeks of the year from April to October, 7 days a week from 9am until 7pm. The club regularly operates at 90% capacity.

The club also employs a manager and a groundskeeper. There is also a clubhouse with vending machines and changing facilities.

1. Vending-machine rental and replenishment costs amount to £200 per week, while the income from the vending machines amounts to £250 per week.
2. The manager is paid £30,000 per annum.
3. The groundskeeper is paid £20,000 per annum.
4. The clubhouse furniture and fittings cost £10,000 and are expected to last 5 years and have a residual value of £1,000 at the end of that time.
5. Heating and lighting of the clubhouse amounts to £2,000 p.a.
6. Administration and advertising expenses amount to £5,000 per year in total.
7. Insurance of the premises costs £500 per quarter.
8. Other expenses amount to £1,600 per annum.
9. Replacement tennis equipment costs £2,500 per year.

You are required to:

1. prepare a statement to show the annual cost of operating the club;
2. calculate the total annual income the club needs to earn for court hire to achieve a target annual net income of £50,000;
3. calculate the average hourly court-hire charge necessary to meet this target.

contd

⚙ EXERCISE 3

Jock's Tours is a coach company that owns 4 buses, which are available for hire by the hour between 9 am and 5 pm Monday to Saturday for short school excursions. Each bus costs £70,000 and has an estimated life of 6 years, after which it will have a residual value of £10,000. It is also estimated that each bus will cover an average of 400 miles per week and will operate for 52 weeks per year.

The annual running costs are as follows:

1. Drivers' wages – each driver normally works an 8-hour shift for 5 days a week at an hourly rate of £12 per hour and an extra shift on Saturday at an overtime rate of double time. Each driver works 48 weeks and receives 4 weeks' holiday pay at £480 per week.
2. During the drivers' holidays, relief drivers are hired from an agency at a rate of £18 per hour on weekdays and double time on a Saturday.
3. Diesel – fuel consumption of each bus is 10 miles per litre at a cost of £1.00 per litre.
4. Servicing – each bus is serviced every 10,000 miles at a cost of £200 per service.
5. Tyres – a full set of tyres is replaced every 20,000 miles and costs £1,200 per set.
6. Insurance – £1,500 per bus per year.
7. Road tax – £692 per bus per year.
8. In addition, the company incurs administration and marketing costs which amount to £12,000 per quarter.

You are required to calculate:

1. how many miles each bus travels per annum;
2. the total cost of operating each bus per annum;
3. the cost per bus per half-day hire;
4. the charge per bus per half-day hire if a mark-up of 100% is to be added (rounded up to the nearest £10);
5. the total annual operating cost of running the entire service.

⚙ EXERCISE 4

Pete's Eats is a small roadside café used mainly by long-distance lorry drivers and other travellers. The cafe is open every day of the year between 6am and 8pm. The restaurant has a capacity of 1,000 meals per week and works at 80% capacity. Kitchen equipment cost £50,000, has a life of 10 years and will have no residual value at the end of that time.

The following information relates to the annual running costs.

1. On weekdays, the employees consist of 2 chefs and 4 waiting staff, each working a basic 7-hour shift, with a chef and 2 waiting staff working between 6am and 1pm, and the other 3 working between 1pm and 8pm.
2. The chef will be paid £15 per hour and the waiting staff at £7 per hour.
3. At weekends, there are another 2 part-time chefs and 4 part-time waiting staff who all work 2 shifts each at the same rate as the full-time employees.
4. Each employee is entitled to 4 weeks' paid holiday per annum. During holiday periods, temporary staff are employed at the same rate as the staff they are replacing.
5. It is estimated that food and beverage supplies will cost on average £41,268.
6. Insurance is £280 per month.
7. Rent and rates are £420 per month.
8. Other expenses amount to £2,500 per annum.

Calculate:

1. the annual running cost of the café;
2. the total number of meals;
3. the average cost per meal;
4. the average price to be charged per meal based on a 25% mark-up.

ONLINE

Find more exercises on service costing at www.brightredbooks.net

ONLINE TEST

Test yourself on service costing at www.brightredbooks.net

PROCESS COSTING 1

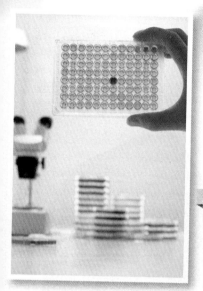

WHAT IS PROCESS COSTING?

Process costing is a method of costing used in manufacturing industries where products are mass-produced and have to go through various processes. For example, chemicals, beer and paint are all products that are identical and need to be passed through various processes before they are complete.

The main aim of process costing is to identify all the costs associated with each process in order to identify a cost per unit for each one. This cost per unit is then used to value the outputs from the process, which are in turn used as inputs to the next process or transferred to the inventory of finished goods.

Example 1:

A product passes through two processes before it is complete. During the month of January Year 1, 1,000 units are produced. The following information relates to the processes:

	Process 1	Process 2
Materials	4,000	3,100
Labour	3,500	2,000
Fixed overheads	1,200	1,500
Variable overheads	1,300	1,400

The costs for a process are known as the inputs and are listed on the debit side of the account as follows:

Process 1 account

	Debit			Credit			Balance		
	Units	Cost per unit	£	Units	Cost per unit	£	Units	Cost per unit	£
Materials	1,000	£4.00	£4,000				1,000	£4.00	£4,000 Dr
Labour		£3.50	£3,500						£7,500 Dr
Fixed overheads		£1.20	£1,200						£8,700 Dr
Variable overheads		£1.30	£1,300						£10,000 Dr
Transferred to Process 2				1,000	£10	£10,000			0

 DON'T FORGET

The costs of a process are known as inputs.

The cost per unit is worked out by adding all the inputs, i.e. £10,000, and dividing by the number of units, i.e. 1,000, as follows:

Cost per unit = 10,000/1,000 = £10 per unit

This is now used to value the output to Process 2, which is recorded in the output side of the account and subsequently entered on the debit side of the Process 2 account, as follows:

Process 2 account

	Debit			Credit			Balance		
	Units	Cost per unit	£	Units	Cost per unit	£	Units	Cost per unit	£
From Process 1	1,000	£10.00	£10,000				1,000	£10.00	£10,000 Dr
Materials		£3.10	£3,100						£13,100 Dr
Labour		£2.00	£2,000						£15,100 Dr
Fixed overheads		£1.50	£1,500						£16,600 Dr
Variable overheads		£1.40	£1,400						£18,000 Dr
Transferred to finished goods				1,000	£18.00	£18,000			0

 DON'T FORGET

The output from one process either goes into the next process or is transferred to stores as finished goods. The inputs from another process are part of the materials cost of a process.

As can be seen from the above Process 2 account, the inputs to the account comprise the 1,000 units from Process 1 together with all the costs of Process 2. Furthermore, the 1,000 units from Process 1 comprise part of the materials cost of Process 2. Therefore the materials cost of Process 2 is £13,100. At the end of the process, the units are now complete and are transferred to the inventory of finished goods to be included in the inventory.

The cost per unit of finished goods is calculated as follows:

$$\frac{\text{Total cost of inputs to Process 2}}{\text{Number of units produced}} = \frac{£18,000}{1,000} = £18 \text{ per unit}$$

contd

NORMAL LOSS AND WASTAGE

In many processes, there can be some loss during the process due to (for example) evaporation, chemical changes or remnants of material left over. These losses are unavoidable during production and have an impact on the cost per unit. For example:

Say 1,000 litres of a chemical are introduced to Process 1 but, during production, 10% is lost due to normal evaporation, and therefore 900 litres of finished product are produced at the end of the process. The inputs to the process are as alongside.

	Process 1
Materials	4,000
Labour	3,500
Fixed overheads	1,200
Variable overheads	300

The process account would look like this:

Process 1 account	Debit			Credit			Balance		
	Units	Cost per litre	£	Units	Cost per litre	£	Units	Cost per litre	£
Materials	1,000	£4.00	4,000				1,000	4.00	£4,000 Dr
Labour		£3.50	3,500						£7,500 Dr
Fixed overheads		£1.20	1,200						£8,700 Dr
Variable overheads		£0.30	300						£9,000 Dr
Normal loss				100	£0.00	£0.00			£9,000 Dr
Transferred to finished goods				900	£10.00	£9,000			0

As you can see from the account above, we are still accounting for the 1,000 litres but have noted that 100 have been accounted for as normal losses. The formula for calculating the cost per unit looks like this:

$$\frac{\text{Total costs}}{\text{Normal output}} = \frac{£9,000}{900} = £10 \text{ per litre}$$

 **DON'T FORGET**

Waste cannot be used and has no value.

SALES OF NORMAL SCRAP

Not all scrap is thrown away. Sometimes it has a value and can be sold. If it can be sold and has a value, it is referred to as spoilage or scrap. If it has no value and needs to be thrown away, it is referred to as wastage or waste. The proceeds of sales of normal scrap are deducted from the total costs before calculating the cost per unit. For example, let us say that the 100 units of normal loss could have been sold for £0.90 per unit. The cost-per-unit calculation would now look like this:

$$\frac{\text{Total costs – Sales of normal scrap}}{\text{Normal output}} = \frac{£9,000 – £90}{900} = \frac{£8,910}{900} = £9.90 \text{ per litre}$$

 **DON'T FORGET**

Spoilage or scrap can be sold and has a value.

The process account would now look like this:

Process 1 account	Debit			Credit			Balance		
	Units	Cost per unit	£	Units	Cost per unit	£	Units	Cost per unit	£
Materials	1,000	£4.00	4,000				1,000	4.00	£4,000 Dr
Labour		£3.50	3,500						£7,500 Dr
Fixed overheads		£1.20	1,200						£8,700 Dr
Variable overheads		£0.30	300						£9,000 Dr
Normal loss				100	£0.90	£90.00			£8,910 Dr
Transferred to finished goods				900	£9.90	£8,910			0

 **DON'T FORGET**

Normal losses reduce the number of good units produced and increase the cost per unit.

 ONLINE

Head to www.brightredbooks.net to complete the exercises on process costing.

 ONLINE TEST

Test yourself on process costing at www.brightredbooks.net

 THINGS TO DO AND THINK ABOUT

1. Describe a situation where it would be appropriate to use process costing.
2. Outline the main aim of process costing.
3. Explain how normal loss affects the cost per unit.
4. Explain the difference between wastage and spoilage.

PROCESS COSTING 2

ABNORMAL LOSSES

Unlike normal losses, abnormal losses are not an expected result under normal circumstances and are dealt with differently from normal losses. These are losses that result from accidents, errors and inferior workmanship. The main difference in accounting for abnormal losses is that they have no effect on the cost per unit calculation. They are transferred to an abnormal loss account and then written off as losses in the Income Statement at the end of the financial period.

Abnormal losses can often be sold – but, whether they can be sold or not, this still does not affect the cost per unit. All accounting entries relating to the abnormal loss are dealt with in the abnormal loss account, and any income received only serves to minimise the extent of the overall loss.

Taking the example from the previous page, 1,000 litres are input to Process 1. Normal loss amounts to 10% of input, but due to a spillage only 800 litres of good output are produced. All losses are sold for £0.90 per litre.

The inputs are as follows:

	Process 1
Materials (1,000 litres)	£4,000
Labour	£3,500
Fixed overheads	£1,200
Variable overheads	£300

DON'T FORGET

Sales of normal scrap reduce the cost per unit.

The cost per unit would still be calculated as follows:

$$\frac{\text{Total costs} - \text{Sales of normal scrap}}{\text{Normal output}} = \frac{£9,000 - £90}{900} = \frac{£8,910}{900} = £9.90 \text{ per litre}$$

Here (as before), normal output is still 900 units. The cost per unit is unchanged. However, the process account now looks like this.

Process 1 account	Debit			Credit			Balance		
	Units	Cost per unit	£	Units	Cost per unit	£	Units	Cost per unit	£
Materials	1,000	£4.00	4,000				1,000	4.00	£4,000 Dr
Labour		£3.50	3,500						£7,500 Dr
Fixed overheads		£1.20	1,200						£8,700 Dr
Variable overheads		£0.30	300						£9,000 Dr
Normal loss				100	£0.90	£90.00			£8,910 Dr
Transferred to finished goods				800	£9.90	£7,920			£990 Dr
Abnormal loss				100	£9.90	£990			£0.00

Abnormal-loss account			
	Dr	Cr	Bal
From Process 1 (100 litres @ £9.90)	£990		£990 Dr
Sales of abnormal scrap @ 90p per litre		£90	£900 Dr
Income Statement		£900	£0

The abnormal loss is then debited to an abnormal-loss account, and the sales of scrap are credited, thus reducing the loss to £900. At the end of the financial period, the loss is then transferred to the Income Statement.

DON'T FORGET

Abnormal losses do **not** affect the unit cost of output but result in a write-off to the Income Statement.

WORK IN PROGRESS

At the end of a financial period, there will normally be some products which are started but only partly finished. This is known as work in progress. This work in progress is given a value and needs to be taken into account when calculating the cost per unit.

contd

Example:

During Year 3, Simpson plc produces a product using Process A to which the following figures relate for Year 4.

Process A	
Materials (1000 kg)	£20,000
Labour	£4,000
Fixed overheads	£1,200
Variable overheads	£700

Normal loss: 10% of total input quantity
Closing work in progress: 100 kg costing £500
Completed units transferred to finished goods: 700 kg
All losses are sold for £2 per kg.

Since the work in progress will be completed in the following year, the cost of this will be included in next year's completed production and so will not be included in the cost-per-unit calculation. The formula for cost per unit now looks like this:

$$\frac{\text{Total costs} - \text{Sales of normal scrap} - \text{value of closing work in progress}}{\text{Normal output (i.e. good production} + \text{abnormal loss)}}$$

$$= \frac{£25,900 - £200 - £500}{800} = \frac{£25,200}{800} = £31.50 \text{ per unit}$$

Alternatively, the normal output could be calculated by taking the total input weight and subtracting the WIP and the normal loss. In the above example, this would have been calculated as 1,000 kg – 100 kg – 100 kg = 800 kg.

ONLINE

Head to www.brightredbooks.net to learn some extension material on the calculation of work in progress.

ONLINE

Head to www.brightredbooks.net to complete the exercises on process costing.

EXERCISES ON PROCESS COSTING

EXERCISE 1

A product passes through 2 processes before it is complete. During the month of January Year 1, 1,000 units are produced. The following information relates to the processes:

	Process 1	Process 2
Materials	£8,000	£6,200
Labour	£7,000	£4,000
Fixed overheads	£2,400	£3,000
Variable overheads	£2,600	£2,800

You are required to:
1. Calculate the total cost per kg.
2. Prepare the 2 process accounts.

EXERCISE 2

During Year 1, 1,000 kg of raw materials are entered into Process 1. Normal loss is 10% of input weight, with all losses being sold as scrap for £10 per kg.

The following information relates to Process 1:

	Process 1
Materials	£16,000
Labour	£14,000
Fixed overheads	£4,800
Variable overheads	£6,700

You are required to:
1. Calculate the total cost per kg.
2. Prepare the process account.

EXERCISE 3

During Year 2, 1,000 kg of raw materials are entered into Process 1. Normal loss is 10% of input weight, with all losses being sold as scrap for £10 per kg. During Year 2, only 800 kg of good output is produced.

The following information relates to Process 1:

	Process 1
Materials	£10,000
Labour	£14,000
Fixed overheads	£5,000
Variable overheads	£1,250

You are required to:
1. Calculate the total cost per kg.
2. Prepare the process account.
3. Prepare the abnormal-loss account.

EXERCISE 4

During Year 3, 6,000 kg of raw materials are entered into Process X. Normal loss is 5% of input weight, with all losses being sold as scrap for £1.80 per kg. During Year 3, only 5,200 kg of good output are produced. Closing work in progress amounts to 300 kg and is valued at £1,000.

The following information relates to the processes:

	Process X
Materials	£20,000
Labour	£12,880
Fixed overheads	£2,500
Variable overheads	£450

You are required to:
1. Calculate the total cost per kg.
2. Prepare the process account.
3. Prepare the abnormal-loss account.

ONLINE TEST

Test yourself on process costing at www.brightredbooks.net

THINGS TO DO AND THINK ABOUT

1. Explain the meaning of abnormal loss.
2. Describe how abnormal losses are treated in the accounts.
3. Explain the meaning of 'work in progress'.

BUDGETING AND BUDGETARY CONTROL: SALES BUDGETS

When a plan is expressed quantitatively, it is known as a **budget**; and the process of converting plans into budgets is known as **budgeting**.

BUDGETS AND PEOPLE

Probably in no other part of accounting is there a greater need for understanding other people than in the process of budgeting. Budgets are prepared to try to guide the firm towards its objectives. There is no doubt that some budgets that are drawn up are even more harmful to a firm than if no budget was drawn up at all.

Budgets are drawn up for control purposes, that is, an attempt to control the direction that the firm is taking. Many people, however, look upon budgets not as a guide but as a 'straitjacket'. The following are undesirable actions that can result from people regarding budgets as a straitjacket rather than a guide.

- The sales manager refuses to let a salesperson go to Sweden in response to an urgent and unexpected request from a Swedish firm. The reason – the overseas sales expenses budget has already been spent. The result – the most profitable order that the firm would have received for many years is taken up instead by another firm.

- The works manager turns down requests for overtime work because the budgeted overtime has already been exceeded. The result – the job is not completed on time, and the firm has to pay a large sum under a penalty clause in the contract for the job, which stated that if the job was not finished by a certain date then a penalty of £20,000 would become payable.

BUDGETS AND PROFIT PLANNING

Budgeting is probably accountancy's major contribution to business management.

The main objectives of budgets:

1. Planning

This means a properly coordinated and comprehensive plan for the whole business. Each part of the plan must interlock with the other parts. Left to their own devices, department managers may make decisions about the future which are **incompatible** or even in conflict with other departments. For example, Sales Dept may be planning to extend the credit period in order to stimulate sales to a point beyond the bank overdraft arrangements. Budgeting helps to avoid such conflicts by encouraging managers to consider how their plans affect other departments and how the plans of other departments affect them. This also leads to better communication between departments.

2. Control

Just because a plan is set down on paper does not mean that the plan will carry itself out. Control is exercised via the budgets, thus the name 'budgetary control'. To do this means that the responsibility of the managers and budgets must be so linked that the responsible manager is given a guide to help him/her produce certain desired results, and the actual achieved results can be compared against the expected, that is, actual compared with budget.

contd

3. Participation/motivation

By actively involving managers at all stages of the hierarchy, the process of budgeting brings the different levels closer together. The junior members feel that they have a say in the running of the organisation, and this leads to increased job satisfaction and consequently productivity.

TYPES OF BUDGET

There are three main types of budget:

1. Sales budget
2. Production budget
3. Cash budget.

The sales budget

The **sales budget** is usually the first budget to be prepared, because the sales quantities often affect the preparation of the other budgets. To prepare the sales budget, you will need the following information:

- Opening inventory (units)
- Production units for each month
- Closing inventory (units).

You may only be provided with details of the opening or closing inventory. However, it is important to remember that the closing inventory for one month will be the opening inventory for the next month.

Example:

Sales budget

Sales budget for January to June Year 2

	Jan	Feb	Mar	Apr	May	Jun
Opening inventory	30	40	45	45	50	55
Add purchases	400	400	450	450	500	550
	430	440	495	495	550	605
Less closing inventory	40	45	45	50	55	60
Sales	390	395	450	445	495	545

DON'T FORGET

The three main budgets are:
1. Sales
2. Production
3. Cash.

DON'T FORGET

The closing inventory for one month becomes the opening inventory for the next month.

ONLINE

Remember you can access the SQA past papers online to practise answering exam questions. Follow the link at www.brightredbooks.net

ONLINE TEST

Test yourself on preparing budgets at www.brightredbooks.net

 THINGS TO DO AND THINK ABOUT

1. From the information alongside, prepare the sales budget for the 6-month period July–December Year 2 for Smiths Ltd.

   Hint: The opening inventory for August must have been the closing inventory for July.

	Year 2						Year 3
	Jul	Aug	Sep	Oct	Nov	Dec	Jan
Production	5,000	2,300	4,500	6,000	3,900	4,200	6,000
Opening inventory	250	450	600	350	420	500	650

2. From the information alongside, prepare the sales budget for the 6-month period July–December Year 2 for Young's plc.

	Year 2						Year 3
	Jul	Aug	Sep	Oct	Nov	Dec	Jan
Production	6,000	3,500	5,200	8,000	5,600	6,300	7,600
Opening inventory	255	550	700	450	580	700	620

3. From the following information, prepare the sales budget for Scott's plc for the 6-month period January–June for Year 1.

	Jan	Feb	Mar	Apr	May	Jun	Jul
Production	18,000	16,500	18,450	21,550	14,800	15,600	16,750
Opening inventory	2,000	1,500	1,820	1,400	1,500	1,820	2,250

BUDGETING AND BUDGETARY CONTROL: PRODUCTION BUDGETS

THE PRODUCTION BUDGET

The purpose of a production budget is to ascertain how many units should be produced by the business each month. A production budget is usually prepared from the information contained in the sales budget. To prepare the production budget, you will need the following information:

- Closing inventory (units)
- Sales units for each month
- Opening inventory units.

Example:

Production budget for January to June Year 2

	Jan	Feb	Mar	Apr	May	Jun
Sales	1,000	1,200	1,400	1,600	1,800	2,000
Less opening inventory	800	960	1,120	1280	1,440	1,600
	200	240	280	320	360	400
Add closing inventory	960	1,120	1,280	1,440	1,600	1,760
Production	1,160	1,360	1,560	1,760	1,960	2,160

UNEVEN AND EVEN PRODUCTION FLOWS

An even production flow usually arises when sales are even over a year. For example, the demand for, and sales of, many electrical products rarely fluctuate from month to month, and so an even production flow can be maintained.

DON'T FORGET

An even production flow means that the same quantity of goods are produced each month.

DON'T FORGET

An uneven production flow means that different quantities are produced each month.

Example: Even production flow

Suppose sales for the first 6 months are budgeted to be as follows:

Jan	Feb	Mar	Apr	May	June
20	30	60	80	70	40

There has to be an **even production flow** of **50 units** per month.
Closing inventory each month **must not** fall below **100 units**.
The problem here is to find the **inventory level** that the firm would need on **1 January**.

Solution:

The opening inventory can be found by trial and error. For instance, if you decided to see what would happen if the firm started off with 100 units of inventory at 1 January, you would find that, after adding production and deducting sales each month, the inventory level would fall to **90 units in May**. This is shown below.

	Jan	Feb	Mar	Apr	May	Jun
Opening inventory	100	130	150	140	110	90
+ even production	50	50	50	50	50	50
	150	180	200	190	160	140
Less sales	20	30	60	80	70	40
Closing inventory	130	150	140	110	**90**	100

As **100 units** of inventory is the minimum needed each month, you would need to start off on 1 January with **110 units**. This is shown in the next table.

contd

	Jan	Feb	Mar	Apr	May	Jun
Opening inventory	**110**	140	160	150	120	100
+ even production	50	50	50	50	50	50
	160	190	210	100	170	150
Less sales	20	30	60	80	70	40
Closing inventory	140	160	150	120	**100**	110

However, some firms by their very nature will have uneven production levels, and this will be accepted by their labour force. An ice-cream firm would find sales at the highest level in summer, tailing off in winter. It is not really possible to build up inventory of ice-cream very much in the winter for summer sales! Even if it could be done technically, the cost of refrigerating large quantities of ice-cream for several months could hardly be economic. Such a firm will normally have a far greater relationship between current inventory levels and current sales than a firm which has even production levels.

ONLINE

Find all the answers to the questions and exercises in this book at www.brightredbooks.net

ONLINE TEST

Head to www.brightredbooks. net to test yourself on preparing budgets.

 THINGS TO DO AND THINK ABOUT

1. From the following information, prepare the production budget for Menzies Ltd for the 6-month period January–June Year 1.

	Jan	Feb	Mar	Apr	May	Jun	Jul
Sales	6,000	6,500	7,000	6,200	4,300	5,400	5,800
Opening inventory	600	650	700	500	520	580	700

2. From the following information, prepare the production budget for Donald Craig Ltd for the 6-month period July–December for Year 1.

	Year 1						Year 2
	Jul	Aug	Sep	Oct	Nov	Dec	Jan
Sales	8,500	9,700	10,200	10,800	7,800	8,100	9,000
Opening inventory	900	950	1,100	680	810	780	710

3. For the year ended 31 December, the sales of units are expected to be:

Jan	70	May	30	Sept	60
Feb	90	Jun	20	Oct	70
Mar	60	Jul	20	Nov	90
Apr	40	Aug	30	Dec	50

The opening inventory at 1 January will be 120 units. The closing inventory at 31 December will be 150 units.

(a) Prepare a production budget to show opening inventory, production and closing inventory per month if an even production flow is required and inventory levels during the year could be allowed to fall to zero.

Hint:

$$\frac{\text{(Closing inventory + Total sales for the 12 months) – Opening inventory}}{\text{12 months}}$$

(b) Given the same information plus the constraint that inventory levels must never fall below 110 units, and that extra production will be undertaken in January to ensure this, what will the January production figure be?

4. A firm wants to maintain an even production flow for the first 6 months followed by an even production flow of 20 units per month greater for the last 6 months.

Opening inventory of units at 1 January 50
Closing inventory of units wanted at 31 December 120
Sales of units during the year 620

How many units should be manufactured per month:

(a) January to June
(b) July to December?

5. Prepare a production budget to show what the production levels would have to be for each month if the following data was available:

(a) Inventory levels wanted at the end of each month: Jan 690, Feb 780, Mar 1,100, Apr 1,400, May 1,160, Jun 940 units.
(b) Expected sales each month: Jan 800, Feb 920, Mar 1,090, Apr 1,320, May 1,480, Jun 1,020 units.
(c) The inventory level at 1 January will be 740 units.

BUDGETING AND BUDGETARY CONTROL: CASH BUDGETS

CASH BUDGETS

It is no use budgeting for **production** and for **sales** if, sometime during the budget period, the business runs out of cash funds. Cash is therefore also budgeted for, so that any shortage of cash can be known in advance and action taken to obtain permission for a loan or a bank overdraft to be available then, rather than wait until the shortage or deficiency occurs.

The finance needed may not just be by way of borrowing from a bank or finance house; it may well be a long-term need that can only be satisfied by an issue of shares or debentures. Such issues need to be planned well in advance, and a cash budget can reveal (a) that additional funds may be needed, (b) how much is needed and (c) when it will be needed.

TIMING OF CASH RECEIPTS AND PAYMENTS

In drawing up a cash budget, it must be borne in mind that all the payments for units produced would very rarely be at the same time as production itself. For instance, the raw materials might be bought in March, incorporated in the goods being produced in April, and paid for in May. On the other hand, the raw materials may have been in hand for some time, so that the goods are bought in January, paid for in February, and used in production the following August. Contrary to this, the direct labour part of the product is usually paid for almost at the same time as the unit being produced. Even here, a unit may be produced in one week and the wages paid one week later, so that a unit might be produced on, say, 27 June, and the wages paid for the direct labour involved might be paid on 3 July.

Similarly, the date of sales and the date of receipt of cash will not usually be at the same time, except in many retail stores. These goods might be sold in May and the money received in August, or even paid for in advance so that the goods might be paid for in February but the goods not shipped to the buyer until the end of May. This is especially true, at least for part of the goods, when a cash deposit is left for specially made goods, which will take some time to manufacture. A simple example of this would be a made-to-measure suit on which a deposit would be paid at the time of order, the final payment being made when the completed suit is collected by the buyer.

LAYOUT OF A CASH BUDGET

Cash budgets are better prepared on a spreadsheet.

McMillan Ltd cash budget for March–June Year 2	March	April	May	June
	£	£	£	£
Opening balance	12,000	47,200	69,000	48,000
Receipts				
Retail cash sales	40,000	35,000	30,000	20,000
Credit sales – 1 month	30,000	25,000	25,000	10,000
Credit sales – 2 months	20,000	10,000	12,000	5,000
Any other income	10,000	8,000	4,000	2,000
Total receipts	100,000	78,000	71,000	37,000

contd

Payments				
Purchases – deposit 20%	8,000	6,000	10,000	4,000
Purchases – balance 80%	32,000	24,000	40,000	16,000
Selling expenses	2,000	2,000	4,000	4,000
Labour	15,000	18,000	20,000	10,000
Bonus	2,000		2,000	
Variable expenses	800	1,200	1,000	600
Fixed costs	5,000	5,000	5,000	5,000
New fittings			10,000	10,000
Total payments	64,800	56,200	92,000	49,600
Closing balance	47,200	69,000	48,000	35,400

Solution:

Grants Ltd						
Cash budget for January–June Year 3						
	Jan	Feb	Mar	Apr	May	Jun
	£	£	£	£	£	£
Opening balance	3,200	3,045	2,920	2,420	1,545	780
Receipts						
Credit sales	960	1,080	840	1,200	720	1,440
Total receipts	960	1,080	840	1,200	720	1,440
Payments						
Materials	520	560	600	480	640	680
Labour	300	330	390	420	450	360
Variable expenses ¾	150	165	195	210	225	180
Variable expenses ¼	45	50	55	65	70	75
Fixed expenses	100	100	100	100	100	100
Motor van				800		
Total payments	1,115	1,205	1,340	2,075	1,485	1,395
Closing balance	3,045	2,920	2,420	1,545	780	825

Example:

Prepare a cash budget for Grants Ltd for the 6 months ended 30 June Year 3, to be drafted from the following information:
1. Opening cash balance at 1 January Year 3 is £3,200.
2. Units sell at £12 each, cash received 3 months after the date of sale.

Year 2			Year 3								
Oct	Nov	Dec	Jan	Feb	Mar	Apr	May	Jun	Jul	Aug	Sep
80	90	70	100	60	120	150	140	130	110	100	160

3. Production in units:

Year 2			Year 3								
Oct	Nov	Dec	Jan	Feb	Mar	Apr	May	Jun	Jul	Aug	Sep
70	80	90	100	110	130	140	150	120	160	170	180

4. Materials used in production cost £4 per unit of production. They are paid for 2 months before being used in production.
5. Direct labour: £3 per unit, paid for in the same month as the unit produced.
6. Other variable expenses: £2 per unit, ¾ of the cost being paid for in the same month as production, the other ¼ paid in the month after production.
7. Fixed expenses of £100 per month are paid monthly.
8. A motor van is to be bought and paid for in April for £800.

 **DON'T FORGET**

Depreciation costs do not involve any actual movement of cash, and so they do not appear in a cash budget. Depreciation involves writing down the value of an asset, but there is no actual payment of cash for depreciation.

 ONLINE

For more exercises on cash budgets, head to www.brightredbooks.net

 ONLINE TEST

Test your knowledge of this topic at www.brightredbooks.net

THINGS TO DO AND THINK ABOUT

S. Grant has exactly £10,000 cash with which to start a business. Her plans for the first 6 months' trading are:

1. Payments for goods and supplies: Jan £5,600, Feb £7,100, March £9,200, April £10,700, May £9,400, June £6,400.
2. Trade receivables will be: Jan £4,100, Feb £5,600, March £8,000, April £7,200, May £7,300, June £8,800.
3. Loan receivable on 1 March: £800, to be repaid in full plus £100 interest on 1 June.
4. Drawings per calendar month: £250.

You are required to draw up a cash budget for the 6 months, showing the opening and closing balances each month.

EXAM-STYLE EXERCISES ON BUDGETING AND BUDGETARY CONTROL

PREPARING BUDGETS

Try out this exercise on preparing a combined production and cash budget before attempting exam-style exercises 2 and 3.

 **EXERCISE 1**

The following estimates have been prepared for Taylors Ltd:

1. Cash and cash equivalents on 1 June to be £50,000.
2. Sales for the 6-month period April–September:

April	May	June	July	Aug	Sept
6,000	7,000	6,400	7,000	7,600	6,600

3. Unit selling price to regular trade customers is to be £55.
4. All sales are on credit, and cash discount for payment within 1 month is 5%.
5. On average, 50% of customers make payment 1 month after sales. The remaining customers pay 2 months after sales. The firm estimates that, of those customers taking longer than 1 month to pay, 1% will result in a bad debt.
6. End-of-month inventory levels will be 800 units for March, April and May, rising to 1,000 units in June and July. In August they will fall back to 800.
7. Raw materials are paid for 2 months after production. The cost is £35 per unit.
8. Direct labour is £12 per unit and is paid in the same month as the units are produced.
9. A production bonus of £2 per unit is paid for in any month where production exceeds 6,800 units. The bonus is paid the following month.
10. Variable production costs amount to £4 per unit and are paid in the month incurred.
11. Monthly fixed costs are estimated to be £30,000, including depreciation of £8,000.
12. A loan for £25,000 was received in August.
13. Taylors Ltd intends to replace its fleet of cars for the sales force in June at a cost of £100,000. A deposit of £40,000 will be paid in June and the remainder in 10 equal instalments starting in July.

<u>You are required to:</u>

1. Prepare the production budget for the 6 months April–September.
2. Calculate the unit selling price for '1 month' customers and for '2 month' customers.
3. Prepare a monthly cash budget for the 3 months June–August.
4. From your cash budget, state whether Taylors Ltd will experience a cash-flow problem during the 3-month period.
5. If so, suggest 1 reason for this and how it could be overcome.

 DON'T FORGET

If completing this exercise on a spreadsheet, point 9 should make use of an IF statement.

 ONLINE

For an exercise combining a sales and cash budget, head to www.brightredbooks.net

Advantages of preparing budgets	Disadvantages of preparing budgets
1. Budgets ensure that business activity has been carefully planned by the owners or managers.	1. Budgets can act as a straitjacket – and, as a result, important but unexpected opportunities can be turned down.
2. Budgets provide a basis for monitoring actual activity against forecasts.	2. Budgets can demotivate staff if the targets set are too challenging or if the staff feel the targets (sales or production) have been imposed upon them.
3. Budgets enable expenditure to be controlled more effectively.	3. Budgets can also be undemanding of staff, so that targets can be easily achieved and so the business's true potential is not fully realised.
4. Budgets ensure that business activity is coordinated.	

SPECIMEN EXAM-STYLE EXERCISES

⚙ EXERCISE 2

The following estimates have been prepared by Victor Enterprises plc.

1. Cash and cash equivalents on 31 August Year 3: £40,000.
2. Number of units to be produced:

July	Aug	Sept	Oct	Nov	Dec
2,000	3,000	2,500	4,000	1,550	3,500

3. Unit inventory levels at the end of each month are:

June	July	Aug	Sept	Oct	Nov	Dec
300	500	300	800	400	450	950

4. Unit selling price is to be £30, less 10% trade discount, less a further discount of 5% for spot cash.
5. Credit sales are to account for 80% of each month's total sales.
6. Credit customers are to settle their accounts 2 months after the month of sale, bad debts being on average 2.5%.
7. Raw materials used in each month's production are to be paid for the following month. The cost is to be £5 per unit, less 15% trade discount.
8. Variable production overhead costs of £2 per unit are to be paid in the month incurred.
9. Direct labour of £15 per unit is to be paid in the same month as the unit is produced. A bonus of £5 per unit produced, in excess of a monthly quota of 2,500 units, is to be paid the following month. (Show the bonus payment separately from the basic labour payment.)
10. New equipment costing £30,000 is to be purchased in September and paid for in 4 equal monthly instalments starting in October.
11. Monthly fixed costs, excluding depreciation of £600, are to be £2,400.

1. **Calculate** the number of units to be sold to meet the forecast production and changes in inventory levels for each of the 6 months, July to December.
2. **Prepare** a monthly cash budget for the 3 months, September to November.

⚙ EXERCISE 3

The following estimates have been prepared by Ambers Ltd.

1. Cash and cash equivalents on 30 June Year 4: £5,000.
2. Number of units to be sold:

	May	June	July	August	September
Credit	3,000	4,000	4,300	4,400	3,800
Cash	400	500	600	700	500

3. Unit selling price: £20, less 5% for spot cash.
4. Credit customers to settle their accounts by the end of the month following the month of sale, bad debts being on average 6%.
5. Unit inventory levels at the end of each month:

April	May	June	July	August	September
1,200	1,350	1,550	1,450	1,650	1,500

6. Variable unit costs:
   Materials £2; labour £8; production overhead £4; selling overhead £2.
7. Materials suppliers to be paid 2 months after the materials are used in production.
8. Wages to be paid in the month the units are produced.
9. Variable production overhead to be paid in the month incurred.
10. Variable selling overhead to be paid in the following month.
11. Monthly fixed costs, including depreciation of £1,000, to be £3,400.
12. New machine costing £25,000 to be purchased in August and paid for in September.

1. **Calculate** the number of units to be produced to meet the forecast sales and changes in inventory levels for each of the 5 months, May to September.
2. **Prepare** a monthly cash budget for the 3 months ending 30 September.
3. **Comment** on possible alternative arrangements Ambers Ltd might make in respect of financing the acquisition of the new machine.

THINGS TO DO AND THINK ABOUT

1. Describe the main three objectives of budgeting.
2. Using an example, explain how a budget could become a 'straitjacket'.
3. Name the three main budgets prepared by most large firms.
4. Explain the difference between an even production flow and an uneven production flow.
5. Explain why depreciation is not included in a cash budget.
6. Describe the main advantages and disadvantages of preparing budgets.

Task

Outline some of the benefits of using spreadsheet software to prepare budgets.
You should present your findings in a short PowerPoint presentation.

 ONLINE TEST

Head to www.brightredbooks.net to test yourself on preparing budgets.

DECISION-MAKING: CONTRIBUTION ANALYSIS 1

Rent is an example of a fixed cost

FIXED AND VARIABLE COSTS

You will already be aware that fixed costs are those costs which do not vary directly with the level of production, such as rent, whereas variable costs vary directly with the level of production, such as direct materials.

The **total cost** is represented by the **fixed costs** plus **variable costs**.

Some costs comprise a combination of fixed and variable elements. For example, an electricity bill has a standing charge which is fixed per month and then you pay for the electricity you use on top of that. These costs are referred to as semi-variable costs.

Direct materials are a variable cost

TOTAL COSTING

This is where the fixed cost is absorbed into the product on a unit-by-unit basis. For example, the following data relates to a company producing 10,000 units per annum.

Example:

Selling price per unit:	£30
Variable costs per unit:	£20
Total fixed costs for the year:	**£40,000**

The fixed costs per unit would be calculated as follows:

$$\frac{\text{Total fixed costs}}{\text{No. of units produced}} = \frac{£40,000}{10,000} = £4 \text{ per unit}$$

The total cost per unit would be £20 + £4 = £24. Therefore the profit per unit would be calculated as follows:

Selling price	£30
Less total costs	£24
Profit	**£6**

DON'T FORGET

Total cost = fixed costs + variable costs.

However, there are problems arising from taking this approach.

Given that fixed costs remain the same regardless of the level of production, the more you produce the lower the cost per unit. For example, using the same figures as the example above:

No. of units produced	10,000	20,000	40,000
Variable costs per unit	£20	£20	£20
Fixed costs	£40,000 per annum		
Total cost	£240,000	£440,000	£840,000
Cost per unit	£24	£22	£21

Inventory valuation can also be problematic if fixed costs are included in the cost-per-unit calculation. Given that closing inventory is deducted from the cost of production and included in the following period's costs of production, this means that each unit includes an element of costs that were incurred (and probably paid) in the previous accounting period, such as rent.

Fixed costs are also referred to as period costs because they vary with time and not production. It is therefore sensible to write these off against the income for the period in which they are incurred.

contd

Variable cost

The variable cost is described as the cost of making **one** unit. Consider this example:

Variable costs	£10 per unit
Fixed costs	£5,000 per annum

If we produce one unit, the total cost is equal to £10 + £5,000 = £5,010.
If we produce two units, the total cost is equal to £20 + £5,000 = £5,020.

Therefore the cost of making one more unit is actually only £10 since the fixed costs have remained the same, and the increase in total cost is actually the increase in variable costs.

Contribution

However, the fixed costs still need to be paid and still constitute part of the cost of producing the good or service. This is done by calculating the contribution we make from selling each product towards paying off our fixed costs. This is done by subtracting the variable cost from the selling price as follows.

Example:

Selling price per unit	£30
Variable cost per unit	£20
Contribution per unit	£30 – £20 = £10

This means that every unit we sell of this product contributes £10 towards paying off the fixed costs. Using the same example, we can then work out the profit or loss for any volume of production. So, with the following additional information we can draw up a profit statement.

Fixed costs	£15,000
Total units produced	6,000

Profit statement for 6,000 units

Sales	£180,000	→ (6,000 × £30)
Less variable costs	£120,000	→ (6,000 × £20)
= Contribution	£60,000	→ (either 6,000 × £10 or £180,000 – £120,000)
Less fixed costs	£15,000	
= Profit	£45,000	→ £60,000 – £15,000

The contribution per unit represents the increase in profit from selling another unit. In the example above, 6,000 units were sold, returning a profit of £45,000. Look what happens when one more unit is sold.

Example:

Profit statement for 6,001 units

Sales	£180,030	→ (6,000 × £30)
Less variable costs	£120,020	→ (6,000 × £20)
= Contribution	£60,010	→ (either 6,000 × £10 or £180,030 – £120,020)
Less fixed costs	£15,000	
= Profit	£45,010	→ £60,010 – £15,000

The overall profit has increased by £10, i.e. the contribution from selling one more unit.

 THINGS TO DO AND THINK ABOUT

1. Outline the difference between a fixed cost and a variable cost.
2. What is the variable cost of a product?
3. How is contribution calculated?
4. Describe two problems associated with including fixed costs in the cost of a product.
5. What is a semi-variable cost? Give two examples.

 **DON'T FORGET**

Fixed costs do not vary with the level of production.

 **DON'T FORGET**

Fixed costs must be paid even if you do not make or sell any products.

 **DON'T FORGET**

Contribution means contribution towards paying off fixed costs.

 **DON'T FORGET**

Variable costs vary with production whereas fixed costs vary with time.

ONLINE

Head to www.brightredbooks.net for some further exercises on contribution analysis and decision-making.

 ONLINE TEST

Test yourself on contribution analysis at www.brightredbooks.net

EXERCISES ON CONTRIBUTION ANALYSIS

DON'T FORGET

Another name for contribution is 'marginal profit'.

DON'T FORGET

Sales – Variable costs = Contribution

DON'T FORGET

The word marginal means 'one more'.

DON'T FORGET

Contribution – Fixed costs = Profit

EXERCISE 1

The following data relates to the manufacturing of product A:

Selling price	£20
Variable costs per unit	
Materials	£10
Labour	£3
Variable overheads	£2
Fixed costs per annum	£7,500

You are required to calculate:

1. the variable cost per unit
2. the contribution per unit

3. the profit or loss on sales of:
   (a) 1,000 units
   (b) 5,000 units.

EXERCISE 2

The following data relates to the manufacturing of product X:

Selling price	£10
Variable costs per unit	
Materials	£4
Labour	£2
Variable overheads	£1
Fixed costs per annum	£75,000

You are required to calculate:

1. the variable cost per unit
2. the contribution per unit

3. the profit or loss on sales of:
   (a) 10,000 units
   (b) 20,000 units
   (c) 30,000 units.

EXERCISE 3

From the following information, calculate for each product:

1. the variable cost per unit
2. the fixed cost per unit
3. the total cost and profit per unit

4. the contribution per unit
5. the total contribution and profit or loss if all units are sold.

Product	A	B
Selling price	£30	£20
Variable costs		
Direct materials	£12	£10
Direct labour	£5	£3
Variable overheads	£3	£2
Fixed costs per annum	£50,000	£30,000
No. of units produced	10,000	10,000

EXERCISE 4

Damshot Ltd makes two products, A and B. The following data relates to production and sales in Year 1.

	Product A	Product B
Sales (units)	5,000	8,000
Selling price per unit	£50	£40
Raw materials per unit (kg)	2	4
Labour hours per unit	3	2
Raw material price per kg	£3	£2
Wage rate per labour hour	£10	£10

Variable overheads recovery rate is £3 per direct labour hour.

Fixed costs for the year are £25,000.

contd

You are required to calculate:

1. the variable cost per unit for each product
2. the contribution per unit for each product
3. the total contribution for each product
4. the overall profit for the company for Year 1.

EXERCISE 5

The following data relates to a manufacturer who owns 3 factories in Glasgow, Aberdeen and Inverness.

	Glasgow	Aberdeen	Inverness
Production (units)	5,000	5,000	5,000
Selling price	£40	£20	£10
Variable costs per unit			
Materials	£20	£12	£3
Labour	£6	£3	£2
Variable overheads	£4	£3	£1
Fixed costs per annum	£15,000	£15,000	£15,000

You are required to calculate the total profit or loss for each factory.

EXERCISE 6

The following data relates to the manufacturing of product A:

Selling price	£35
Variable costs per unit	
Materials	£14
Labour	£6
Variable overheads	£5
Fixed costs per annum	£30,000

You are required to calculate:

1. the variable cost per unit
2. the contribution per unit
3. the profit or loss on sales of:
   (a) 1,000 units
   (b) 5,000 units.

EXERCISE 7

The following data relates to a firm producing a single product – Product X.

	5,000 units
Sales	£100,000
Less variable costs	£75,000
Contribution	£25,000
Fixed costs	£20,000
Profit/Loss	£5,000

You are required to calculate:

1. the selling price per unit
2. the variable cost per unit
3. the contribution per unit
4. the total profit if 12,000 units were sold.

EXERCISE 8

From the following information, calculate for each product:

1. the total cost and profit per unit
2. the variable cost per unit
3. the contribution per unit
4. the total contribution and profit or loss if all units are sold.

Product	A	B
Selling price	£45	£32
Variable costs		
Direct materials	£16	£20
Direct labour	£8	£3
Variable overheads	£6	£2
Fixed costs per annum	£72,000	£64,000
No. of units produced	8,000	8,000

ONLINE

Head to www.brightredbooks.net for some further exercises on contribution analysis.

ONLINE TEST

Test yourself on contribution analysis at www.brightredbooks.net

DECISION-MAKING: CONTRIBUTION ANALYSIS 2

THE IMPORTANCE OF CONTRIBUTION ANALYSIS

Given that the main aims of business include **profit maximisation**, **survival** and **growth**, it is essential that these outcomes are planned for and not left to chance. Companies can plan for changes in circumstances, market conditions or availability and prices of raw materials, as well as shortages of raw materials, labour or machine time.

It is vital that detailed records are kept regarding sales, demand and costs of production in order that any decisions made are accurate. This information can be historical data based on actual performance, or projected data based on market conditions and research.

Examples of the decisions that are normally based on analysis of variable costs and contribution include:

- the decision to close an unprofitable department or halt production of a product
- the decision to alter the product mix due to a limiting factor
- the decision to accept or reject a special order
- the decision to make or buy a product or component.

Example – Decision to halt production of a product or close a department, branch or factory (or not)

Companies are always looking at the profitability of products, departments or even branches, and will not continue to invest in areas of the business that do not look as though they are financially viable. However, the right course of action is not always obvious, and an analysis of the contribution can make the management think again.

Norcroft Electronics make three products – electronic cars, robots and pets. They are considering halting production of the toy that shows the least profit. The data relating to each toy is as follows:

	Cars	Robots	Pets
No. of units produced per year	10,000	10,000	10,000
	£	£	£
Unit selling price	30	10	38
Variable cost per unit	20	5	18

Fixed costs for the year are £100,000.
Calculate the effect this would have on the total profit for the year, and advise Norcroft plc whether or not they should halt production.

contd

Solution:

First, we need to work out exactly how much profit or loss the company is making.

	Cars	Robots	Pets	Total
No. of units produced per year	10,000	10,000	10,000	
	£	£	£	
Sales	300,000	100,000	380,000	
Variable costs	200,000	50,000	180,000	
Contribution	100,000	50,000	200,000	350,000
Fixed costs				100,000
Profit/loss				250,000

Under the current proposal, production of robots would be halted, since they are showing the lowest contribution.

Second, we need to work out what change in profits that would bring about for the company.

	Cars	Robots	Pets	Total
No. of units produced per year	10,000	0	10,000	
	£	£	£	
Sales	300,000	0	380,000	
Variable costs	200,000	0	180,000	
Contribution	100,000	0	200,000	300,000
Fixed costs				100,000
Profit/loss				200,000

DON'T FORGET

Any decrease in contribution will result in a proportionate decrease in profit.

The overall profit for the company has decreased by £50,000. This is because the sales of robots were contributing £50,000 towards the fixed costs of the company. Closing down production of the robots means that overall contribution has decreased to £300,000 – and, since fixed costs have remained the same, there has been a corresponding drop in profits of £50,000. Therefore closing down the production of robots would not be a good idea unless we could find something else more profitable to invest in.

THINGS TO DO AND THINK ABOUT

1. Outline two of the main aims of business where contribution analysis could be useful.

2. Describe two examples of the decisions that are normally based on analysis of variable costs and contribution.

3. Explain what is meant by the statement 'Fixed costs do not vary with the level of production – they vary with time'.

4. Describe the main aim of contribution analysis.

5. Explain why a company would continue to invest in a product that is making a total loss.

ONLINE

Head to www.brightredbooks.net for further exercises on decision-making.

ONLINE TEST

Test yourself on decision-making at www.brightredbooks.net

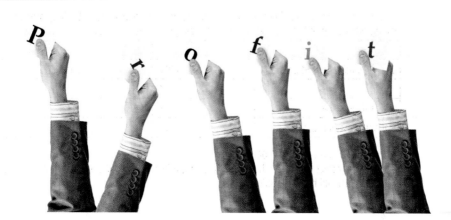

DECISION-MAKING: CONTRIBUTION ANALYSIS 3

LIMITING FACTORS

Under normal circumstances, the most profitable product is the one with the highest contribution per unit. In this case, the company would try to make and sell as many of these products as people would be willing to buy. However, there are certain situations where this is not the case. For example, say demand for a product was 10,000 units but the firm cannot make 10,000 units due to one of the inputs to the process, such as skilled labour, being in short supply. This is known as a **limiting factor** or **key factor**. Other examples of limiting factors are machine hours, materials or even space in the factory.

When a limiting factor is present, the most profitable product is the one that yields the highest contribution per unit of the limiting factor. This is expressed as contribution per labour hour, contribution per machine hour or contribution per kg of material etc. This is worked out by first calculating the contribution per unit and then dividing that by the number of units of the limiting factor it takes to make one unit. For example, each of the following three products has a different limiting factor which is then used to work out the contribution per unit of that limiting factor.

Example – Decision to alter the product mix to maximise profits due to a limiting factor

Product	A	B	C
Limiting factor	Labour hours	Machine hours	Material
Contribution per unit	£24	£16	£12
Units of limiting factor per unit produced	3 labour hours	4 machine hours	2 kg of material
Contribution per unit of limiting factor	£8 per labour hour	£4 per machine hour	£6 per kg of material

ANSWERING EXAM QUESTIONS WITH A LIMITING FACTOR

A typical exam question will offer several products with the same limiting factor. Candidates are usually asked to rank products in order of profitability and allocate a product mix that will maximise profits. For example:

A company produces three products using the same production process. The factory is currently working at full capacity. However, due to a shortage of machine hours, it is impossible to meet customer demand for all three products, so they are currently producing 5,000 units of each.

The data relating to each product is as follows:

Product	X	Y	Z	Total
Contribution per unit	£35	£25	£20	
Machine hours per unit	5	5	2	
Current production (units)	5,000	5,000	5,000	
Total contribution	£175,000	£125,000	£100,000	£400,000
Fixed costs				£100,000
Total profit				£300,000

The actual market demand for each product is as follows:
Product X – 6,000   Product Y – 6,500   Product Z – 7,000.
You are required to advise the company of the product mix that will maximise profits.

contd

Step 1 – Work out how many hours they have available at full capacity by multiplying the number of hours it takes to make each product by the number of products produced, as follows:

Product X – 5,000 units × 5 hrs = 25,000 hours
Product Y – 5,000 units × 5 hrs = 25,000 hours
Product Z – 5,000 units × 2 hrs = 10,000 hours

Total hours available = 25,000 + 25,000 + 10,000 = 60,000 hours.

Step 2 – Work out the contribution per machine hour for each product by dividing the contribution per unit by the number of machine hours it takes to produce one unit, as stated in the question.

Product	X	Y	Z
Contribution per unit	£35	£25	£20
Machine hours per unit	5	5	2
Contribution per machine hour	£7	£5	£10

As can be seen from the table above, product Z is now the most profitable product, as it yields the highest contribution per machine hour.

Step 3 – Decide on the order of production, i.e. in what order to allocate the scarce resource of machine hours. As per this table:

Product	X	Y	Z
Contribution per machine hour	£7	£5	£10
Order of production	2	3	1

Step 4 – Work out how many units of each product the company can produce using its limited resources, starting with the most profitable, i.e. product Z.

Demand for product Z = 7,000 units

Hours required to produce 7,000 units = 7,000 x 2 hrs per unit = 14,000 hours

This leaves 60,000 – 14,000 = 46,000 hours to allocate to the production of less profitable products.

Product X is the next most profitable, therefore look at how many hours are required to produce all of the demand for this product, i.e.:

Demand for product X = 6,000 units

Hours required to produce 6,000 units = 6,000 × 5 hrs per unit = 30,000 hours

This leaves 46,000 – 30,000 = 16,000 hours to allocate to the production of product Y.

Starting with the number of hours we have, i.e. 16,000, now work out how many units of Y we can produce within this allocation.

Hours required to produce 1 unit of Y = 5

Therefore we can produce 16,000 ÷ 5 = 3,200 units of Y

Step 5 – Now work out the new total contribution and profit.

Product	X	Y	Z	Total
Contribution per unit	£35	£25	£20	
Production	6,000	3,200	7,000	
Total contribution	£210,000	£80,000	£140,000	£430,000
Fixed costs				£100,000
Total profit				£330,000

Therefore by altering the product mix we have increased the total profit by £30,000 to £330,000.

 DON'T FORGET

Limiting factors can include labour, materials, floor space or machine hours.

 DON'T FORGET

The most profitable product is the one which gives the highest contribution per unit of the limiting factor.

ONLINE

Head to www.brightredbooks.net for further exercises on decision-making.

 THINGS TO DO AND THINK ABOUT

1. Explain how the total cost and profit per unit are calculated.
2. Identify two disadvantages of including fixed costs in the total cost of a product.
3. Describe a situation where a decision might be made to keep producing a product that is showing a loss.
4. Explain the meaning of the term 'limiting factor'.
5. Describe how you would calculate the contribution per unit of the limiting factor. Illustrate your answer with an example.

ONLINE TEST

Test yourself on decision-making at www.brightredbooks.net

DECISION-MAKING: OPPORTUNITY COST

OPPORTUNITY COST

Opportunity cost is an economic concept that regards the true cost of anything as the next best alternative foregone. For example, if you wanted a holiday and a car but could only afford one, the true cost of the car is the holiday you gave up to get it.

Similarly in accounting, when you make the decision to allocate resources to product A and take them away from product B, then the contribution lost from product B forms part of the cost of making product A.

Example 3 – Decision to accept a special order (or not)

Following on from the example on the previous page, let us say that the company has been approached with a special order for 100 units of product X at a reduced selling price of £55. Should the company accept the special order?

Product	X	Y	Z	Total
Selling price	£70	£60	£50	
Variable costs	£35	£35	£30	
Contribution per unit	£35	£25	£20	
Machine hours per unit	5	5	2	
Contribution per machine hour	£7	£5	£10	
Production	6,000	3,200	7,000	
Total contribution	£210,000	£80,000	£140,000	£430,000
Fixed costs				£100,000
Total profit				£330,000

There are several ways of looking at this, but they will all point towards the same answer, which will be either to accept or to reject the order.

Method 1

Since both units require 5 hours, we can just substitute one unit of X for one unit of Y. However, if both products took a different amount of time to produce, we would have to use the contribution per machine hour to work out the opportunity cost.

	£
Selling price of special order	55
Less variable costs	35
Contribution per unit	20
Less opportunity cost per unit of Y (lost contribution)	25
Loss per unit of special order	(5)

contd

DON'T FORGET

Opportunity cost is what we need to give up in order to get something.

DON'T FORGET

Opportunity cost is defined as 'the next best alternative foregone'.

Method 2

	£
Sales of special order (100 x £55)	5,500
Less variable costs (100 x £35)	3,500
Total contribution	2,000
Less opportunity cost of Y (5 hrs x 100 = 500 hrs x £5)	2,500
Loss	(500)

Method 3

	£
Selling price of special order	55
Less variable costs	35
Contribution per unit	20
X sales	100
Notional profit	2,000
Less opportunity cost	2,500
Loss	(500)

All three methods point to the fact that, for every unit of the special order you produce, you are losing £5 – and this can be expressed as a loss of £5 per unit, or £500 overall. Either way, the order should be rejected.

Example 4 – Decision to make a component or buy it in

Another question where the concept of opportunity cost comes into play is the decision to make or buy a component in the production process.

The following data relates to a product made in a factory that is working at full capacity and currently buys in a component for £45 per unit. The company is considering making the component, and estimates that it will take 1 labour hour at a total variable cost of £25 per unit. Advise the company whether they should make or continue to buy in the component.

	£	£
Selling price		200
Less variable costs		
Materials	70	
Labour (3 hrs @ £10 per hr)	30	
Variable overheads	10	110
Contribution		90

Since we are told that the factory is working at full capacity, the 1 hour required to produce the component will reduce the hours available for production of the finished product, and the contribution that is normally made from this hour is therefore the opportunity cost. The cost of making this component is therefore:

Contribution per labour hour of the finished product = £90 ÷ 3 = £30
Add the variable costs of making the component = £25
Total cost of making the component = £30 + £25 = £55
Current cost of buying the component = £45
It will therefore cost an extra £10 to make the component, so the company should continue to buy in the component.

DON'T FORGET

Opportunity cost is the contribution lost from switching to another product or course of action.

DON'T FORGET

Always remember to add the opportunity cost to the variable costs when deciding whether to make or buy.

ONLINE

Head to www.brightredbooks.net for further exercises on decision-making.

ONLINE TEST

Test yourself on decision-making at www.brightredbooks.net

 THINGS TO DO AND THINK ABOUT

1. Identify two situations where contribution analysis is used for decision-making.

2. Explain what is meant when it is said that a firm is working at full capacity.

3. Explain what is meant by the term 'opportunity cost'.

4. Describe in detail how the opportunity cost of switching from one product to another is calculated.

EXERCISES ON DECISION-MAKING

EXERCISE 1

A company has 3 branches and is considering closing down any branch that shows a loss. The data relating to each branch is as follows:

	Glasgow	Edinburgh	Aberdeen
Units sold	5,000	7,000	8,000
Selling price	49	40	35
Variable costs			
Materials	2	10	5
Labour	33	22	20
Overheads	3	5	1
Labour hours	3	2	2

Fixed costs amount to £90,000 and are recovered on the basis of labour hours.

1. You are required to calculate for each product:
   (a) the fixed cost per unit
   (b) the variable cost per unit
   (c) the profit or loss per unit.
2. The company is considering closing down any branch that is making a loss which will reduce fixed costs by £5,000. Sales at the other 2 branches will remain at the same level.
   (a) Calculate the total profit if this course of action is adopted.
   (b) Advise the company whether or not they should close the branch, giving a reason for your answer.

EXERCISE 2

A company produces 3 products using the same production process. The factory is currently working at full capacity. However, due to a shortage of machine hours, it is impossible to meet customer demand for all 3 products, so they are currently producing 6,000 units of each.

The data relating to each product is as follows:

Product	A	B	C	Total
Contribution per unit	£50	£40	£36	
Machine hours per unit	10	5	4	
Current production (units)	6,000	6,000	6,000	
Total contribution	£300,000	£240,000	£216,000	£756,000
Fixed costs				£180,000
Total profit				£576,000

The actual market demand for each product is as follows:

Product A – 7,000 units Product C – 8,000 units.
Product B – 8,500 units

You are required to advise the company of the product mix that will maximise profits.

EXERCISE 3

A company makes 3 products, A, B and C. They have been approached with a special order for 200 units of product A at a reduced selling price of £45. Should the company accept the special order?

Product	A	B	C	Total
Selling price	£60	£50	£52	
Variable costs	£27	£30	£33	
Contribution per unit	£33	£20	£19	
Labour hours per unit	3	2	2	
Production	6,500	4,100	5,000	
Total contribution	£214,500	£391,500	£95,000	£430,000
Fixed costs				£90,000
Total profit				£301,500

EXERCISE 4

The following data relates to a product made in a factory that is working at full capacity and currently buys in a component for £20 per unit. The company is considering making the component and estimates that it will take 1 labour hour at a total variable cost of £10 per unit. Advise the company whether they should make or continue to buy in the component.

	£	£
Selling price		100
Less variable costs		
Materials	35	
Labour (3 hrs @ £5 per hr)	15	
Variable overheads	5	55
Contribution		45

EXERCISE 5

Wilson plc makes 2 products and is currently working at 80% capacity.

The following information relates to production for Year 1.

	Product A	Product B
Sales (units)	10,000	12,000
Selling price per unit	£71	£56
Raw materials per unit (kg)	3	2
Labour hours per unit	4	3
Raw material price per kg	£5	£4
Wage rate per labour hour	£10	£10

Variable overheads recovery rate is £2 per direct labour hour.

Fixed costs for the year are £75,000.

contd

You are required to calculate:

1. the variable cost per unit for each product
2. the contribution per unit for each product
3. the total contribution for each product
4. the overall profit for the company for Year 1
5. the total number of labour hours currently being used
6. the total number of labour hours available at full capacity.

The company has commissioned some market research and discovered that the market demand for each product is as follows:

Product A – 14,000   Product B – 16,000.

7. Given that fixed costs will remain unchanged and there is no limit to the supply of raw materials, how many units of each product should be made at full capacity in order to maximise profits?
8. Calculate the total profit from this product mix.

During Year 2, the business will be working at full capacity. If the business is approached by a customer to produce 100 units of Product B at a special price of £48 per unit:

9. Advise whether or not to accept this special order.

 EXERCISE 6

A company has 3 departments and is considering closing down any department that shows a loss. The data relating to each department is as follows:

Department	X	Y	Z
Units sold	3,000	5,000	6,000
Selling price	60	40	30
Variable costs			
Materials	2	8	6
Labour	30	20	20
Overheads	3	4	2
Machine hours	3	2	2

Fixed costs amount to £62,000 and are recovered on the basis of machine hours.

1. You are required to calculate for each product:
   (a) the fixed cost per unit
   (b) the variable cost per unit
   (c) the profit or loss per unit.
2. The company is considering closing down any department that is making a loss which will reduce fixed costs by £6,000. Sales in the other 2 departments will remain at the same level.

(a) Calculate the total profit if this course of action is adopted.
(b) Advise the company whether or not they should close the department, giving a reason for your answer.

 EXERCISE 7

A company produces 3 products using the same production process. The factory is currently working at full capacity. However, due to a shortage of labour hours, it is impossible to meet customer demand for all 3 products, so they are currently producing 7,000 units of each.

The data relating to each product is as follows:

Product	A	B	C	Total
Contribution per unit	£27	£42	£60	
Labour hours per unit	3	6	12	
Current production	7,000	7,000	7,000	
Total contribution	£420,000	£294,000	£189,000	£903,000
Fixed costs				£220,000
Total profit				£683,000

The actual market demand for each product is as follows:

Product A – 8,000 units   Product C – 7,500 units.
Product B – 9,000 units

You are required to advise the company of the product mix that will maximise profits.

 EXERCISE 8

A company makes 3 products, X, Y and Z. They have been approached with a special order for 300 units of product Y at a reduced selling price of £25. Should the company accept the special order?

Product	X	Y	Z	Total
Selling price	£30	£40	£50	
Variable costs	£12	£22	£36	
Contribution per unit	£18	£18	£14	
Labour hours per unit	3	2	2	
Production	5,000	4,100	5,000	
Total contribution	£90,000	£73,800	£70,000	£233,800
Fixed costs				£60,000
Total profit				£173,800

ONLINE

Head to www.brightredbooks.net for further exercises on decision-making.

ONLINE TEST

Test yourself on decision-making at www.brightredbooks.net

THINGS TO DO AND THINK ABOUT

1. Describe how the variable cost of a product is calculated.
2. Explain how contribution analysis could be used to make decisions.
3. Describe the relationship between the contribution per unit and the total contribution.
4. Explain how the overall profit is calculated using contribution analysis.
5. Explain why it might be problematic to separate fixed and variable costs.

INDEX